SID 821
SIS 823
518

KT-435-384

Advanced Practical Sociology

Nick Howe

Nelson

Thomas Nelson & Sons Ltd
Nelson House Mayfield Road
Walton-on-Thames, Surrey
KT12 5PL   UK

51 York Place
Edinburgh
EH1 3JD   UK

Nelson Blackie
Wester Cleddens Road
Bishopbriggs
Glasgow
G64 2NZ   UK

Thomas Nelson (Hong Kong) Ltd
Toppan Building 10/F
22a Westlands Road
Quarry Bay Hong Kong

Thomas Nelson Australia
102 Dodds Street
South Melbourne
Victoria 3205 Austrialia

Nelson Canada
1120 Birchmount Road
Scarborough Ontario
MIK 5G4 Canada

© Nick Howe 1994

First published by Thomas Nelson and Sons Ltd 1994

ISBN 0–17–448218–3
NPN 9 8 7 6 5 4 3 2 1

Printed in China

ACKNOWLEDGEMENTS

The author and publishers wish to thank the following who have kindly given permission for the use of copyright material:

Bloomsbury Publishing Limited for an extract from *Cocaine Kids* by Terry Williams, 1990.

The Guardian for extracts from the television and radio guide, 1993.

Penguin Books Ltd for extracts from *Hell's Angels* by Hunter S. Thompson (Penguin Books, 1967), copyright © Hunter S. Thompson, 1966, 1967.

Peters, Fraser and Dunlop for an extract from *Folk Devils and Moral Panics* by Stanley Cohen, 1973.

CONTENTS

INTRODUCTION

PRESENTATION 98

ANSWERS AND COMMENTS ON EXERCISES 111

INTRODUCTION

The task ahead: As you read this you will be embarking on one of the most substantial coursework projects you have so far encountered. That remark is not designed to intimidate you, but to stress the need for careful thought before you begin. Each section of this guide is designed to steer you through each stage of the project, and it is written from my direct, recent experience of working with A level students on their projects. Follow these stages carefully and the task ahead will become an enjoyable challenge.

The first section on page 7, Basic Facts About the Project, will answer most of the questions you have at this starting point. Looking at it from where you are now, what is the main advantage of the project? The answer is twofold. First, it accounts for 25% of the mark scheme, which means that by April of your second A level year (when the project has to be submitted) you can be well on the way to passing an A level in Sociology before even having taken an exam. This means that you will have a shorter Paper 2 – two essay questions must be answered in one and a half hours, better than four in three hours. You will still need good essay writing skills, but doing the project certainly reduces the final examination pressure.

Second, it is a great opportunity. An opportunity to take an area of sociology that interests you and actually contribute to that area of knowledge; to conduct a research inquiry into an issue or problem that may not even have been explored before by any sociologist. It is certainly clear from my experience of guiding students through the project, and from marking them, that a lot of satisfaction can result from such original work.

On the first point – the shorter Paper 2 examination – it should also be said that students taking the project option obtained slightly higher grades that those who did not.

This book is designed to help you gain that higher grade. It follows the stages on the project as you will experience them, and so gives you advice and structure as you proceed if you read each section as your work reaches that point. To begin, I suggest you read the section that follows this as it should answer immediate queries most students have at the outset. You could then begin the idea generating exercises in the following chapter, to get underway as soon as possible.

Note on Examination Boards

Students using this text should be aware of its primary, though not exclusive focus on the type of coursework project demanded by the Associated Examining Board (AEB) A level Sociology Project Option. This does not mean that the principles of, and encouragement to, good sociological practice contained in the following chapters cannot be applied to other examination board assessment schemes. Nor does it mean that the candidate should narrowly focus on producing work to the mark scheme. Rather, the emphasis is on producing high quality original (primary) or secondary research material and organising its final presentation in a coherent and rational fashion. References in the text to a mark scheme can broadly be taken to be in line with the AEB one for the project, but such comments and exercises are relevant to any student-centred sociological enquiry and should hence have a cross examination centre relevance.

CHAPTER 1

BASIC FACTS ABOUT THE PROJECT

Some of the information below is drawn from AEB project guidelines, but most comes from my own answering of student questions before project work begins. All are worthy of consideration at the opening stages of approaching the project option.

How Long Should the Project be?

The AEB recommend very close to 5000 words in total; any less and a full attempt at the mark scheme may not occur, substantially more than 5000 words and more time than necessary may be spent on the project. The Chief Examiner recalled moderating one project in the first year the project option was available that topped 25,000 words. Although it was above degree level in quality and length, and gained a top grade by a large margin, he seriously questioned the knock-on effect on that student's other A level work (and, indeed, on their time for other areas of the sociology syllabus). I myself have marked projects in excess of 10,000 words which, while excellent, could have gained equal marks and been considerably less time consuming.

Message: keep very close to 5000 words. One issue is how best to apportion these through the various sections of the project. This will vary somewhat depending on the project. For example, a series of four or five highly qualitative, in-depth unstructured interviews will yield much prose data, and so this particular student's Content section (where the research results are presented) will be much longer than another student's, who may only have two or three pages of largely graphical data presentation.

Table 1 below gives a broad idea of how long each section should be, and also explains what is in each section. More advice and detail on each section follows in chapters ahead.

Section of project	Contents	Approximate length (words)
1 Rationale	Statement of the area and aims of the project, including the hypothesis and what methods will be used.	600
2 Context	An outline of the existing sociological material surrounding the hypothesis. Relate this material to the hypothesis.	1200
3 Methodology	Here it is stated which methods will be used and why. Present and justify in detail (for example, why certain questions were asked in an interview) and say what went wrong. What weaknesses does the chosen method have? Could alternatives be used?	1200
4 Content	The presentation of the findings, either by written prose (for very qualitative data) or in tables, graphs, pie-charts, etc. Computer graphics can be very impressive here, but are not essential.	900
5 Evaluation	A key section in which the conclusions are drawn from the research.	900
6 Bibliography	A list of the sources used in the project.	200
		Total 5000

Table 1

Some minor adjustment for a particular project may be necessary, and no-one will quibble with 200 or 300 words either side of 5000, but it is strongly advised to be close to that final total.

Can My Project be About Anything I Like?

Not quite. There is great freedom to choose the area and the hypothesis, from within broad guidelines. Basically the following affect the choice:

a It must be ethical and legal. Hence, it is not possible to engage in any dubious participant observation which may lead to difficulties with the police or others. It is also necessary to be careful when considering topics for interviews or questionnaires.

Areas such as child abuse, suicide and rape are very sensitive, and must be considered thoughtfully. This does not rule them out of bounds, but means certain distinctions must be made. For example, interviewing victims of child abuse is out of bounds by the AEB's Ethics Guide for the project – what is possible is to, for example, interview a random sample of the public on their attitudes to dealing with child abusers. Generally, the AEB Ethics Guide says that: 'In many guises, social research intrudes into the lives of those studied. While some participants in social research may find the experience a positive and welcome one, for others it may be disturbing.' Due care and sensitivity are required, as is confidentiality: 'The anonymity and privacy of those who participated in the research process should be respected. This may mean changing respondents' names and, in some cases, place names too.'

b The project must be syllabus-relevant: this means the tutor or lecturer must agree that the student's chosen area of study falls within the A level sociology syllabus, and is hence permitted by the board. The final approval for a hypothesis rests with the tutor/lecturer in any case, so a student should not proceed without close consultation with him or her.

If project work is being done in another related field of social science at A level – for example, Psychology – it is possible to do research work on a hypothesis applicable to both, though ultimately two separate pieces of work have to be submitted for each relevant subject. For more information on choosing a topic, there is a series of practical exercises on page 22.

c Practical constraints: time and cost. William Foot Whyte spent from 1937 to 1940 researching the Italian street corner gang for his classic PO study *Street Corner Society*; more recently, Terry Williams spent part of each week from 1982 to 1986 with crack cocaine sellers in Harlem and the Bronx, New York City, to do the fieldwork for *The Cocaine Kids* 1990. Young and Lea's (1986) sample for their pioneering victim surveys in the study of crime contained a total of 11,000 people. Such a large victim survey (where people are asked what crime they have been the victim of) is sociolgically commendable, but beyond the means of a single student.

Time and resources of this kind are not available to the A level student, so over-ambition at the outset must be avoided. Somewhere between thirty and fifty is a valid questionnaire sample (properly selected, of course), and for some projects researching a very qualitative issue (such as women's changing experience of childbirth and childcare this century) ten or so unstructured interviews will be sufficient. Participant Observation (PO), often mistakenly thought of as the most 'user-friendly' of research techniques, actually requires considerable thought and support, and the cost, time, advisability and ethics of a covert PO study will need to be carefully considered. This does not mean it cannot be done, and done well; what it does require is a very clear set of reasons why PO is the best way of researching the hypothesis. PO should not be chosen and then a hypothesis found to fit the method, rather the hypothesis should be defined before the method(s) to research it are selected.

Can a Group Project be Done?

Technically the board does allow this, although the final write up and submission must be done individually. I would not recommend group projects, although individual tutors/lecturers may feel otherwise. Tensions can arise over how and in what way the research should proceed, and resentments occur if one or two people sit back and do not pull their weight (what psychologists call 'social loafing'). There is an advantage to be gained in group projects in that they enable larger sample bases to collect data from, but this has to be balanced against the factors mentioned above. Further, the sense of satisfaction at completing the project is arguably a very personal one. Apart from anything else, most students might choose to do a group project with friends, and that in itself is often not a good idea – it is desirable to still remain friends at the end of the course.

However, group projects can promote different skills of co-operation and collaboration which could be desired, and much professional research is carried out by groups. Hence, this choice is very much a personal one.

Can I Refer to Previous Coursework?

It is best not to. The AEB board's guidelines, 'Malpractice in A/AS level Coursework' (1991) state quite clearly that 'using people's work from previous years' is among one of the most serious cases of malpractice and will result in the disqualification of the candidate. Other general warnings are not to copy from other students' work, from text books or other books, and to acknowledge all sources. Also avoid 'excessive outside help'. Basically this means the project must:

a   Be the candidate's own individual work.
b   Use, not copy from, other sources.

How Long do I Have to do the Project?

The project must be done in the last twelve months of the course, but as it has to be submitted by April 30th of the second year this effectively gives from June of the first year to the following April: about ten months.

This sounds like a lot of time to produce a 5000 word project, but time must be thoughtfully planned or a last minute rush can occur near April. There are always other pressures anyway, from other A level coursework, holidays, homework, practice examinations – those students who wait for a clear period in which to do their sociology project find it never materialises.

The tutor/lecturer should normally make some of the class contact time available for project work, which is very useful for consultation on areas where you need clarification. This time becomes more useful as the deadline draws near, so it may be that the tutor/lecturer increases this nearer to April.

How Different Will it be to GCSE Type Coursework?

In that an inquiry is being originated and conducted, not so different. The depth will however differ, and the A level project demands the use of concepts and theories far more than GCSE level. The A level project is also, at 5000 words, longer than most GCSE projects which generally fall between 1500 and 3000 words.

How Much Help Can My Teacher Give Me?

What s/he cannot do is outline what the hypothesis should be and how it should be researched. The tutor/lecturer is someone with sound sociological knowledge who can:

a   Respond to ideas being thought of.
b   Check the accuracy of sociological statements made, and the conclusions drawn from the research.
c   Ask questions which may help to get a student's work unstuck or gain a new direction, rather than say what should be done.

On the coursework marksheets that are sent to the board for each candidate it asks the student and tutor to sign that the coursework is the 'result of the independent effort of the candidate except where indicated'. It is obviously better if no indication of help (outside that defined above as acceptable) needs to be recorded.

How Many Hours a Week Should be Spent on the Project?

To work steadily through until April, around three hours a week, of which one will possibly be in class time. This is only a very rough guide, and is certainly a minimum; it is based on how much work outside class would go into two essay topics over this time from September to April, which is what would be done if not doing the project. Remember, too, that at certain points in the project (such as collecting data or analysing findings) more time will be needed.

Do I Have to Choose a Topic Already Studied?

No, it is possible to look at other topics on the A level syllabus that are available (and which may not even be done in class by the end of the course). This will involve extra work as knowledge of the topic will be mostly self-taught; the tutor/lecturer may not feel this is the best approach, so do consult carefully if in doubt. I should say, though, that I have taught at least two students who have produced very good quality projects on topics not studied in class time, but it did require a bit more self-discipline and self-motivation on their part.

This section should hopefully have answered most preliminary questions about the project. A thorough review of the coursework option from the viewpoint of the student which would repay reading is by Heaton and Andrew in Vol.2, No.4 of *Sociology Review* 1993, pp 26–8. The authors interviewed fourteen students who had completed the project option about the experience. The article contains much practical advice, direct from students who have learnt by recent personal experience.

It is now time to begin the practical business of devising a working hypothesis or problematic.

CHAPTER 2

GENERATING RESEARCH IDEAS

The process of generating research ideas is an essential forerunner to a successful enquiry overall. This does not always mean that the sociologist proceeds with a firm or even specifically worded hypothesis, but may have a loosely phrased or broad concept framework to work from.

Phenomenology and Positivism

There is a methodological distinction in sociological research along two broad lines. First, the phenomenological, which enquires into how the detail of social life is constructed and maintained. This often has as a characteristic the notion that research interests and focus can develop alongside the research as it happens. This type of approach often, although not exclusively, tends towards the more ethnographic (concerned with small-scale study of behaviour) research approaches such as participant observation and/or unstructured or discursive interview techniques. It is precisely these very flexible approaches that can discover new elements of a sociological concept as an enquiry progresses, and hence new aspects become apparent to the researcher and come to be included in the research. Examples of this type of sociology are discussed in Researching Phenomenologically, p. 17.

A second broad approach is that which derives from the positivist tradition. This has its origins in the early work, in the nineteenth century, of Auguste Comte and later the formidable contribution of Emile Durkheim to the development of sociology as a distinct discipline. This earlier sociological tradition purports that sociology can have a scientific approach and use research to seek reasonably firm causal relationships between social phenomena. Durkheim's study of suicide (*La Suicide*, 1897) was in exactly this tradition, searching as it did for formal and verifiable relationships between an individual's social connectedness with others and their exposure to the probability of suicide. To summarise a complex argument extremely briefly, Durkheim claimed to have conclusively proved that a balance of social integration and of individuality was essential for healthy social membership – too much involvement (what he termed altruism) or too little involvement (termed egoism) would have a strong probability of causing suicide. This latter kind of approach is much more likely, although not exclusively so, to make use of a testable statement – a proposition or hypothesis that the research will test to ascertain its validity. For example, Durkheim asserted that 'suicide varies inversely with the degree of integration of the groups of which the individual forms a part', and this he claimed to have proved to be correct by his very quantitative methods. Suicide operated by a law of social integration, comparable with more conventional scientific laws such as gravity and evaporation, both of which occur only under certain conditions and not others. Thus there is a body of sociological work based on the notion that sociology can be scientific in its procedures, or follow what is called the hypothetico-deductive technique. This approach is explored in more detail in Researching in a Positivist Manner, p. 21.

Before going further, however, it is instructive at this point to develop more fully the distinction between these two approaches in sociology – the phenomenological and the positivist, or structural theory approach as it is more widely called now.

Structural theorists argue that sociology can be scientific (as in Durkheim's approach above) and that it can and should follow an ideal of science in its procedures. Many phenomenologists or interpretive sociologists would argue that sociology cannot and should not follow this idea of science. Set out below are some of the main differences in approach between these two views under four main headings:

1   The nature of the subject matter – this means what the sociologists concerned think about how humans behave, as humans are the subject matter of sociology.
2   The aim of sociology – this means what guides the research into the social world. What are we trying to discover about the social world?
3   The methods to be used – here there is a broad distinction between the two approaches which will be developed with brief examples.
4   The desirability or possibility of value freedom – this refers to how much it is possible for sociologists to remain objective or neutral in their research work, or whether it is inevitable that some of their values and judgements will affect it.

1 The nature of the subject matter

Structural theorists stress that in the same way that objects in the natural world are largely inanimate and controlled by external stimuli, so is the social world. Humans are seen as largely passive and as influenced to act in certain ways by forces beyond their control. This view would broadly suggest that just as when a ball is kicked it will travel so far depending on the force of the kick, so if working conditions are altered for a group of workers so will attitudes and output alter.

For phenomenologists, the subject matter of sociology and of the natural sciences (such as physics and chemistry) is very different. Humans are active beings who interpret the world and give meaning to it. Behaviour is not a product of external stimuli but of interpretations and meanings given to an event. Hence, it is not working conditions which affect attitude and output (as structural theorists maintain above), but how these are interpreted and the meanings given.

2 The aim of sociology

Structural theorists argue that the aim is to uncover laws which govern behaviour. The classic example, already referred to, is Durkheim's law about suicide. Such laws are held to be no different from the laws of natural science. For example, there is no difference between:

a   Heat causes water to evaporate.

b Material deprivation (a poor home environment, etc.) causes poor educational attainment.

In both cases, a cause and effect relationship is sought from natural and social life.

For phenomenologists the aim of sociology is to describe, explain and understand the way people interpret the world and the meanings they give to it. Weber in the *Protestant Ethic and the Spirit of Capitalism* (see pp. 416–8 Bilton 2nd Edition, or pp. 659–63 in Haralambos 3rd Edition for a slightly more detailed account of this major study of religion) did not look for 'laws' about why capitalism developed as a structural theorist would – but instead he tried to understand how a belief in Calvinism would affect people's behaviour. Weber attempted to understand the viewpoint of a protestant believing s/he would go to hell if not one of the chosen, and to further imagine what forms of behaviour (for example, prudent and 'moral' social behaviour) this could result in. This is not to seek a 'law' but to imagine the experiences of others in a sociological context.

Similarly, Cicourel in his study of police stereotypings tries to understand the meanings the police give to particular types of behaviour or social characteristics, such as being young, male and black– a category Cicourel found was generally regarded with some suspicion by many police officers.

3 The methods to be used

Structural theorists tend to prefer quantitative techniques in their search for causal explanations. Considerable emphasis is placed on reliability. Commonly applied methods include:

(i) Experiments – such as the Hawthorne experiment (1924) where causal relationships were sought between working conditions and productivity by, for example, varying lighting conditions or break times and seeing if it affected output.

(ii) Comparative methods – the most famous example is Durkheim, but many other sociologists have made use of the method. For example, Douglas compared students who had considerable 'parental encouragement' with their schooling, to those who did not, to see if this factor influenced individual pupil attainment.

(iii) Structured interviews – for example, Willmott and Young's attempt to measure the strength of family ties through the quantity of face-to-face encounters.

Phenomenologists tend to prefer qualitative methods because these allow the search for meanings. They allow the sociologist to see the world from the subject's point of view. Such sociologists tend to use less structured methods which allow for the development of rapport, that retain the natural situation and that do not impose the researcher's definition of what is important. Such methods include:

(i) Participant observation – for example, the attempts in the sociology of deviance by Becker, Whyte, Liebow, Cicourel and others to capture the world view of the social actors involved.

(ii) Unstructured interviews – for example, in the sociology of the family, where participant observation is difficult to employ, sociologists like Gavron, Oakley and Bott have used unstructured in-depth interviews to arrive at an understanding of family life (particularly from the viewpoint of women).

(iii) Some social experiments – such as Garfinkel's Studies in Ethnomethodology in which students are involved in disrupting the normal social world in order to uncover the taken for granted assumptions that sustain it (pp. 95–6 in Anthony Giddens Sociology – 1st or 2nd Edition – is very informative on these social experiments).

Generally, phenomenologists emphasise validity: in other words, the extent to which the information obtained is an accurate and true reflection.

4 The desirability or possibility of value freedom

Structural theorists believe it is both possible and desirable to produce sociological analysis which is objective and value free, meaning it is unaffected by the researcher's values or beliefs. They argue that we should 'treat social facts as things' (Durkheim, 1897); they should be treated as phenomena which exist independently of the observer and of the values of the observer.

The attempt by Douglas to measure factors within the home and school which affect educational attainment is an example. For instance, it is argued that the effect of family size, students' health and parental interest can be measured independently of the values of the researcher.

Phenomenologists contest the idea that value freedom is possible, and the issue of whether it is desirable has been debated at some length. It is impossible because we all have values and these will inevitably influence research. For example, we look at the world in particular ways due to our socialisation; hence we tend to be ethnocentric (to view the world from our immediate geographical and cultural place in it). Spender shows how the English language imposes a male-centred view of the world. Moreover, all sociologists will possess political viewpoints which will influence research.

Phenomenologists argue that it is a paradox that sociologists seek to explain the way in which people behave by reference to values and attitudes and yet deny that the very same values and attitudes affect their own work.

Deciding Between a Broadly Phenomenological or Broadly Structural Approach

This exercise is designed to enable a general sense of methodological direction for the student who has read the above and also has the germ of an idea for a project already. Ask of the general project idea if it seems to be a Yes or No answer to the following two sets of questions:

1 Broadly phenomenological

- Is the initial idea trying to understand the complex and active role of human beings? Yes ☐ No ☐
- Will the idea develop an understanding of social phenomena from the viewpoint of those studied? Yes ☐ No ☐
- Is it a broad idea that needs general exploration and/or personal interpretation? Yes ☐ No ☐

An example of such an idea might be: 'What sort of perceptions of the young do the elderly have?'

If the answer is 'Yes' to most or all of these three questions, the research idea is in a broadly phenomenological approach.

Methods to consider:

- participant observation
- non-participant observation
- unstructured or focused interviews
- documents of life
- qualitative content analysis
- diaries
- conversation analysis

These are considered more fully in Chapter 4 – Conducting the Research.

2 Broadly structural

- Is the idea trying to establish cause and effect relationships? Yes ☐ No ☐
- Will the idea establish laws and make predictions? Yes ☐ No ☐
- Does the idea lend itself to a testable statement that describes links (correlations) between variables? Yes ☐ No ☐

An example of such an idea might be:

'The negative views of the elderly towards young people mean that the elderly distrust the young.' (Contrast this example with the one under phenomenology a few sentences above – the difference should be evident in that the first seeks to open up a very general research interest and the second poses the quite specific form of a relationship between negative views and distrust among elderly citizens with regard to the young.)

If the answer is 'Yes' to most or all three of the questions, the research idea is in a broadly structural theory approach. (See Researching in a Positivist Manner on page 21 for developing the idea along these more structurally based lines.)

Methods to consider:

– questionnaires
– structured interviews
– experiments
– quantitative content analysis
– social surveys
– official statistics
– historical materials

These are considered more fully in Chapter 4 – Conducting the Research.

Researching Phenomenologically

Researchers working from the sociological approach defined at the start of this chapter as phenomenological have often proceeded with a quite generally demarcated area of sociological interest. A readily accessible example of this is the approach Ken Pryce took when beginning his research by covert (and sometimes overt) participant observation into the lifestyle of West Indians in the St Paul's area of Bristol in the late 1970s. In fact, Pryce began his research by only having a vague notion of applying the sociological concept of 'lifestyle' to this particular community. His research ends with a very comprehensive book (*Endless Pressure*, 1980) which graphically illustrates the mores of the West Indian community and also categorises certain groups in an original way according to their relationship with the 'mainstream' white-dominated social world (for an excellent brief extract from Pryce's book where he outlines his opening research approach see Mike O'Donnell's *Reader in Sociology*, p. 49 in the 2nd Edition). Ken Pryce was in fact later killed while doing drug research in the West Indies.

In the two extracts that follow, two sociologists who worked on enquiries involving deviant (and usually illegal) activities describe the beginning of their researches. This can illuminate the more general points of phenomenological method made earlier in this chapter, and also show by example how research can proceed without a formal hypothesis. In both cases, the extract is typical of all the methodological comments made in the book by the author in that no fixed or narrowly defined hypothesis is enunciated. Hunter Thompson was aiming to work his way into the Hell's Angel community near where he lived in California in the mid 1960s, to learn about their way of life from the inside. He makes no more specific an explanation of his aims than his attempt to go behind rather over-reacting newspaper headlines about the Hell's Angels to see their behaviour for himself. Terry Williams was engaged in a very similar task when infiltrating the working lives of crack-cocaine sellers, and he describes in the extract printed here some of the general questions he sought to answer, and explains the process of ethnographic research he is pursuing.

It may prove useful to combine a reading of these two extracts with the three points to consider that follow them.

My dealings with the Angels lasted about a year, and never really ended. I came to know some of them well and most of them well enough to relax with. But at first – due to numerous warnings – I was nervous about even drinking.

Some of the outlaws understand this communications gap, but most are puzzled and insulted to hear that 'normal people' consider them horrible. They get angry when they read about how filthy they are, but instead of shoplifting some deodorant, they strive to become even filthier. Only a few cultivate a noticeable body odour. Those with wives and steady girlfriends bathe as often as most half-employed people, and make up for it by fouling their clothes more often. This kind of exaggeration is the backbone of their style. The powerful stench they are said to exude is not so much body odour as the smell of old grease in their crusty uniforms. Every Angel recruit comes to his initiation wearing a new pair of Levis and a matching jacket with the sleeves cut off and a spotless emblem on the back. The ceremony varies from one chapter to another but the main feature is always the defiling of the initiate's new uniform. A bucket of dung and urine will be collected during the meeting, then poured on the newcomer's head in a solemn baptismal. Or he will take off his clothes and stand naked while the bucket of slop is poured over them and the others stomp it in.

These are his 'originals', to be worn every day until they rot. The Levis are dipped in oil, then hung out to dry in the sun – or left under the motorcycle at night to absorb the crankcase drippings. When they become too ragged to be functional, they are worn over other newer Levis. Many of the jackets are so dirty that the colours are barely visible, but they aren't discarded until they literally fall apart. The condition of the originals is a sign of status. It takes a year or two before they get ripe enough to make a man feel he has really made the grade.

Frenchy and the other Angels at the DePau wanted to know if I'd located them by following the smell. Later that night, at the weekly meeting, I noticed that several were wearing expensive wool shirts and ski jackets under their colours. When the bars closed at two, five of the outlaws came over to my apartment for an all-night drinking bout. The next day I learned that one was an infamous carrier of vermin, a walking crab farm. I went over my living room carefully for signs of body lice and other small animals but found nothing. I waited nervously for about ten days, thinking he might have dropped eggs that were still incubating, but no vermin appeared. We played a lot of Bob Dylan music that night, and for a long time afterwards I thought about crabs every time I heard his voice.

That was in early spring of 1965. By the middle of summer I had become so involved in the outlaw scene that I was no longer sure whether I was doing research on the Hell's Angels or being slowly absorbed by them. I found myself spending two or three days each week in Angel Bars, in their homes, and on runs and parties. In the beginning I kept them out of my own world, but after several months my friends grew accustomed to finding Hell's Angels in my apartment at any hour of the day or night. Their arrivals and departures caused periodic alarms in the neighbourhood and sometimes drew crowds on the sidewalk.

One of the worst incidents of that era caused no complaints at all: this was a sort of good-natured firepower demonstration, which occurred on Sunday morning about three-thirty. For reasons that were never made clear, I blew out my back windows with five blasts of a 12-gauge shotgun, followed moments later by six rounds from a .44 Magnum. It was a prolonged outburst of heavy firing, drunken laughter and crashing glass. Yet the neighbours reacted with total silence. For a while I assumed that some freakish wind pocket had absorbed all the sound and carried it out to sea, but after my eviction I learned otherwise. Every one of the shots had been duly recorded on the gossip log. Another tenant in the building told me the landlord was convinced, by all the tales he'd heard, that the interior of my apartment was reduced to rubble by orgies, brawls, fire and wanton shooting. He had even heard stories about motorcycles being driven in and out the front door.

No arrests resulted from these incidents, but according to neighbourhood rumour they were all linked to Hell's Angels, operating out of my apartment. Probably this is why the police were so rarely summoned; nobody wanted to be croaked by an Angel revenge party.

Dr Hunter S. Thompson, *Hell's Angels*, 1966.

This is a story about teenagers who move in a very fast lane, each one trying to be 'the king, making crazy money for as long as I can, any way I can.'

It focuses on the lives of eight young cocaine dealers in New York City. From 1982 to 1986, I spent some two hours a day, three days a week, hanging out with these kids in cocaine bars, after-hours spots, discos, restaurants, crack houses, on street corners, in their homes and at family gatherings and parties.

These studies took me to the Bronx, Harlem and Washington Heights – areas of high unemployment and diminishing resources, especially for young people. But while quality entry-level jobs were disappearing, illegal opportunities were emerging with considerable force because of the growth of a powerful and profitable multi-national drug industry.

The apartment is crowded with teenagers, all wearing half-laced sneakers and necklace ropes of gold. Doorbells ring every few minutes, white powder dusts the table tops; jagged-edge matchbook covers and dollar bills seem to flow from hand to hand. The talk is frenetic, filled with masterful plans and false promises. Everybody has a girl. Everybody has cocaine. Everybody has a gun.

This is a book about kids, cocaine and crack. But it is also a book about work and money, love and deceit, hope and ambition. It describes – as much as possible in their own words – the world of teenage members of a cocaine ring: the way they do business, their neighbourhood, their families, their highs and lows.

When I first came on the teenage cocaine scene, I was apprehensive, even fearful. I knew these young people were volatile and unpredictable, prone to violence, and not inclined to trust adults – or, for that matter, anyone outside their circumscribed world. Yet I wanted to find out about the kids who sold drugs. How did they get into the cocaine business, and how do they stay in it? How transient is their involvement – can they get out of the business? And where do they go if they do? What are the rewards for those who succeed?

The only way to find the answers to these questions was to follow the kids over time, and that is what I did. For more than four years, I asked questions and recorded the answers without trying to find support for any particular thesis. In the process, I found that the truth was embedded in a complex, miniature society with institutions, laws, morality, language and codes of behaviour of its own. I also found young people whose only shield against fear and uncertainty was a sense of their own immortality.

Doing Ethnography

This attempt to provide a rounded dynamic portrait of the kids, their work and their world, relies heavily on a form of research known as ethnography.

An ethnographer tries to describe everyday behaviour and rituals and, in the process, to reveal hidden structures of power. As this technique requires the researcher to build a close relationship with those being studied, it is necessarily slow: days, sometimes weeks, may pass before the ethnographer can even begin to conduct an interview. These interviews are often 'open'; that is, the investigator has key questions in mind, but is willing to let an informant's responses lead to unanticipated areas as these can provide new understandings of the processes under study.

Ethnography also involves careful observation of individuals in their own social setting, and systematic recording of their action and speech. This can include simple quantitative measures, such as noting the sex, age, and ethnicity of participants, or observing a particular routine. For example, in observing cocaine transactions in a bar or apartment, I might count the number of buyers and sellers; record the techniques used to make (or conceal) a sale or use of the drug, the prices paid and the purity claimed; even tally the number of times patrons visit the bathroom, often a favourite place to snort cocaine discreetly.

But ethnographers also record far more subtle information, such as use of language, gestures, facial expressions, style of clothing: and must watch with care to capture exceptional episodes that can be particularly illuminating.

Clearly, detailed and descriptive field notes are essential in this approach, especially as the observer makes every attempt to accurately record the speech of those observed. In my work, this was often very difficult, even after the kids freely welcomed me into their world. For one thing, any tape recording made in the midst of the turbulent business of cocaine would have been unintelligible – there are phones ringing, people coming and going, and often a more or less constant background of family arguments, babies crying, loud music, and other disturbances. In addition, taking handwritten notes during a conversation warps discussion and inhibits the flow of words.

Besides, although the crew fully accepted me and my work, others – their customers, the hangers-on, cocaine groupies – were not necessarily informed about my role: things were fine as long as I was seen as another waiting buyer or a friend; producing a pad or tape recorder would certainly have stirred suspicions. Another compelling reason to avoid behaving like an observer was the potential for violence. With guns openly visible and police raids a real possibility, I felt I had to keep my hands free, my eyes sharp and my mind clear.

For these reasons, I developed a method of jotting down key words or phrases immediately after each visit, and reconstructing conversations or a scene from those notes the next day. (There were a few exceptions: I did take sketchy notes of some private, one-to-one conversations with individuals I had known for years.) It was not unusual to spend a day or more writing up an hour or two of field observations.

Despite such obstacles, more than 1200 hours of field work produced six thick notebooks, including drawings and diagrams covering every nuance of the kids' operation – methods of production and packaging, forms of dealing and the flow of cash – and a great deal of material about the structure of dealing networks and the rituals of cocaine use.

Although I became close to the kids and people in their world, even grew to think of some of them as friends, some important distances could not be breached: for one thing, they were teenagers; for another, while cocaine use is a part of their daily lives, I never consumed any drug stronger than alcohol, and did not participate in any way in the preparation, transport or sale of drugs.

Terry Williams, *Cocaine Kids*, 1990.

Points to consider

(i)   Why did these two researchers choose participant observation?

(ii) What difficulties did they each encounter in using the method?

(iii) Why should these two researchers find it advantageous to work with a general idea rather than a specific hypothesis?

(Guidance comments are in Chapter 6, p. 111.)

Researching in a Positivist Manner

Before looking at the means by which a hypothesis can be obtained, when working on a project idea that involves a more positivist direction, it is advisable to be clear on exactly what a hypothesis is. Mayntz et al offer a succinct and common-sense definition as follows: '...a hypothesis is concerned with the postulation of a relationship between several factors.

Accordingly, the statement that 48% of workers in West Germany have low job satisfaction would not be a hypothesis because all we are saying is simply that a particular set of workers (workers in West Germany) displays a particular characteristic. However, the statement that for West German workers increased wages leads to greater job satisfaction establishes a relationship between two variables, and is consequently a hypothesis' (R. Mayntz et al: *Introduction to Empirical Sociology*, Penguin, 1976).

Finding your hypothesis

So, the student should be aware from studying methodology that a hypothesis is, put at its simplest, a statement to be tested: to be proved correct or refuted.

This does not mean you have to prove your hypothesis to be correct. An equally high scoring project results from carefully researching an issue and finding the results contradict the original statement, or hypothesis. For example, the board gives the following as a possible type of study:

'A comparison of examination results in state and private schools.'

To be a hypothesis this has to be re-phrased into a statement that can be proved to be correct or refuted (proved wrong). For example, it could form the following hypothesis:

Pupils at private schools gain higher examination results than those at state schools because they have greater teacher attention in smaller classes.

This statement can be proved right or wrong, or partially right or partially wrong (it is also legitimate to find only a part of the hypothesis is confirmed by the data collected). However, many questions have still to be considered in testing the above hypothesis:

- How do you measure examination success? Results at GCSE? At A level?
- Do you look at national figures for state and private schools, or one example of each locally? How do you find such data?
- Do private schools have smaller classes? How would you find this out – send for publicity from selected private schools?
- Do you prove smaller classes mean more attention per pupil, by observation of a class for example, or can you reasonably assume this is so?

As can be seen, once an area of interest is found and part of it is re-phrased as a statement, questions immediately arise that lead into how to try and answer the hypothesis. Looking at the hypothesis being used here as an example once more, it is also important to note one other key aspect:

Pupils at private schools gain higher examination results than those at state schools *because* they have greater teacher attention in smaller classes.

If a student were to look at only the first half of this statement she would not be looking at a sufficiently theoretical aspect of the issue for A level work. At A level it is not only important to say what is happening in society (for example, that some priviledged pupils gain better examination results) but to also explore *why* this may be happening (which may, for instance, be because higher teacher attention helps to gain greater understanding and therefore higher examination results). Hence, the final working hypothesis must seek an explanation for a sociological process that can be shown to be taking place.

Looking at some of the examples below, complete the exercises which follow on re-phrasing the topic area as a hypothesis.

Example

Below is an example of how a student can move from having decided on which broad area of sociology to look at, through to the particular part of that topic that is of interest, to finally reach a statement that can be tested by collecting data – a hypothesis.

Area of syllabus	Topic of study
Ethnicity	Ethnic minority groups and housing
Hypothesis	Ethnic minorities live in a poorer standard of housing than the majority of the population due to disadvantages connected with their ethnic origin.

This statement can be tested with the finding of facts, or, put more sociologically, it can be empirically tested. Data could be found from secondary sources (books, articles, etc.) that may confirm the first part of the hypothesis on poorer housing; some interviews, perhaps, with ethnic minority members of the local community may reveal some of the disadvantages that ethnic minorities experience.

It would be necessary to carefully define what was meant by disadvantage, and also think about how to gain a representative sample of the ethnic community who would be willing to discuss such issues.

The exercise below can be carried out with fellow students in order to exchange hypotheses ideas. There are no definitive answers.

Hypothesis phrasing exercise

Area of syllabus	Topic of study
Family	Changing conjugal (roles between husband and wife) roles this century.
Hypothesis	
Gender	An examination of gender stereotyping in children's comics and teenage magazines.
Hypothesis	
Crime / Deviance	An assessment of the accuracy of official criminal statistics.
Hypothesis	
Media	An evaluation of the effect of sexual and violent portrayals on television.
Hypothesis	

Age and Generation   A study of the differences between the experiences of the elderly and other people's expectations of ageing.

Hypothesis

This last exercise has aimed to illustrate the specific differences between an area of broad enquiry which a student may be interested in and the phrasing of an actual hypothesis. Another way to approach this opening process is to answer, as fully as possible, the list of questions below in Figure 1. This effectively forms a self-help questionnaire, and it may be necessary to complete several versions of it before a workable hypothesis emerges.

Hypothesis Questionnaire

1 The topic in sociology I have found most interesting is _____ because _____
_____
_____

2 The area within that topic that I find most exciting or interesting is
_____
_____

3 Within that area of the topic I can think of the following issues that affect people or society:
a _____
b _____
c _____

4 Each of these issues could be researched if expressed as a hypothesis.
Issue a could form the following hypothesis:
_____
_____
_____

Issue b could form the following hypothesis:
_____
_____

Issue c could form the following hypothesis:
_____
_____

5 Say in each case which method(s) of research would be most appropriate. Why do they seem to be the most suitable?
_____
_____
_____

6 What problems might be anticipated with each hypothesis and research method? How might such problems be overcome?
_____
_____

7 Would any secondary data be required? If yes, where could it be obtained?
_____
_____

Figure 1

Below is an example of how a student might fill in these questions as a way of reaching some firm suggestions for a feasible hypothesis. The task after this stage is to take one of the suggestions that this exercise has generated and use it for your project.

Hypothesis Questionnaire

1 The topic in sociology I have found most interesting is
The media because *I am interested in the effect television in particular has on viewers.*

2 The area within that topic that I find most exciting or interesting is
Effects of sexual and violent content.

3 Within that area of the topic I can think of the following issues that affect people or society:
a *Censorship (Controlling what people see).*
b *TV making people sad and frightened.*
c *TV making people violent or aroused.*

4 Each of these issues could be researched if expressed as a hypothesis.

Issue a could form the following hypothesis:
Media images of violence are thought by people to need greater censorship than currently applies.

Issue b could form the following hypothesis:
Much media content makes people sad or frightened, showing the direct effect television has on its audience.

Issue c could form the following hypothesis:
Much media content makes people violent and/or sexually aroused showing the direct effect television has on its audience.

5 Say in each case which method(s) of research would be most appropriate. Why do they seem to be the most suitable?
PO, Case studies etc difficult in media research { *(a) Interview-possibly questionnaire with examples of violence.*
(b) Same-or people to keep diaries of their viewing responses.
(c) Same- "

6 What problems might be anticipated with each hypothesis and research method? How might such problems be overcome?
Difficulty of making a link with (b) and (c) between reaction and cause: is TV responsible for the effect.

7 Would any secondary data be required? If yes, where could it be obtained?
Data on: (i) Effects of research on the media
(ii) Censorship issues.

Figure 2

In this example the student would clearly now be in a position to proceed with background reading directly relevant to the chosen area of study and particularly focused on the chosen hypothesis. However, the student could make certain adjustments to her phrasing of her intentions for the research, and make sure more ambiguous terms or concepts were fully defined and contextualised before proceeding with the actual research. Answer fully the questions below (possible answers are on page 112 to refer to once the exercise is complete) in order to critically consider this example of the hypothesis questionnaire:

Questions

(i) Is this student's enquiry to be about the media or about television? What is the difference between these two and what impact does this have for the project?

(ii) How could hypothesis **b** be re-phrased to apply purely to television content?

(iii) With the issues that the student has identified in Section **3 b** and **c**, are there any words or concepts that would require careful further definition? Why would they require consideration as sociologically (and particularly methodologically) problematic?

(iv) Are the methods the student has considered for each hypothesis somewhat limited? What other methods might be possible for this research aim?

Stages in the research process

Another way to think of this process of beginning with a hypothesis and integrating it with the data gathering throughout the research, is to look at the idealised research procedure many professional researching sociologists use. This seven stage process actually has its origins in the kind of systematic research procedure employed by a scientist in a laboratory, although there is great debate as to whether scientists themselves actually strictly follow these procedures. For this reason the process is described as an idealised summary of the research procedure, but it can nevertheless be used here to set a framework for the selection of a hypothesis that is subsequently properly integrated with appropriate methods of data gathering.

The seven stages in a typical sociological enquiry are as follows:

1 Observation
2 Forming the hypothesis
3 Choosing the method(s)
4 Selecting the sample
5 Gathering the data
6 Analysing and interpreting the data
7 Considering policy implications.

Putting a little more detail now on each of these stages should enable the need for progression from opening ideas to a balanced research inquiry to be emphasised.

1 Observation

This is generally observing through everyday life or studying an area of interest. For example, possible police prejudice towards ethnic minorities may emerge as an area of interest to someone, as might the question as to whether housewives are content in that role to another person. This makes the opening question of the hypothesis questionnaire above particularly important in aiming to focus on the area of enquiry that may interest and motivate a student for their project.

2 Forming the hypothesis

The hypothesis is the proposition or statement put forward to be tested.

To continue one of the examples used immediately above, a researcher may move from a general concern that the police may have prejudices towards ethnic minorities to a hypothesis that:

the police have negative, stereotypical attitudes to black and Asian people (viewing them as lazy, troublemakers etc.) which affect their behaviour to them.

As such, the general observation about a possible social issue has become a specific and testable hypothesis about an aspect of policing.

3 Choosing the method(s)

This involves consideration of which are the most appropriate for the chosen enquiry. The sociologist has a considerable list of methods to choose from; again, with the example used here it may be that participant observation could reveal the most accurate indications of police behaviour towards ethnic minorities, but it may also be the most inaccessible method to use. The researcher cannot actually become or pretend to be a police officer, so a covert participant observation role is ruled out. To adopt an overt observation role may be more practical, but would certainly require Home Office permission as the government department is responsible for the police, and may also alter the behaviour of the particular police interactions observed. An additional consideration must be that participant observation inevitably produces data generated from small samples (it is possible for the researcher to observe only one group at a time) and as such the information gathered may relate only to the sample studied and not to the wider ethnic or police population.

This difficulty in generalising from participant observation or observation samples because of their restricted size would lead a sociologist to consider other possible research methods in the example being used here. These might solve the sample size issue while still involving other methodological complications. For instance, interviews or questionnaires can raise problems of data validity (how truthful people's replies are), especially in such a sensitive area as racial prejudice.

Many studies make use of combined methods, where some of the shortfalls of a method such as participant observation are compensated for by conducting interviews as well, or using a more quantitative research technique such as questionnaires to balance the qualitative data generated by participant observation. This may certainly be an appropriate approach in a student A level project.

4 Selecting the sample

This technical issue is dealt with in more detail in the section on choosing the methodology (see p. 95), but it is sufficient to note at this point that this is normally influenced by who is being studied and how they are being studied.

Hence it is still important that sample selection is integrated with the other procedures chosen for the research.

So the number, rank and location of the police officers selected for interview or questionnaire evaluation would be an important consideration, to avoid gathering responses from untypical or biased individual police officers.

5 Gathering the data

This refers to the actual conducting of interviews, or gathering of material for a case study of an institution or individual. Alongside the subsequent stage of analysing the data, this is often the most time-consuming stage of sociological enquiries.

6 Analysing and interpretating the data

The questions here are primarily: What has been learnt? Is the hypothesis confirmed or not? What are the trends illustrated?

7 Considering policy implications

Policy refers to the actions that institutions or governments take in dealing with an identified issue. In the example here, if the research were to uncover a level of police prejudice towards ethnic minorities, what should be done? This is how social research can lead to social policy, in that:

- Social theories (such as functionalism) ask why social life is as it is.
- Social research asks what the position is in society at any given moment.
- Social policy asks how government or other institutions should then deal with any issues raised by the research.

With a student A level project the policy implications are inevitably limited – a government minister is unlikely to read the end result – but the Evaluation section of a good project would certainly consider what the policy implications of the research findings are. The main linkage of concern, then, is between the theoretical background to the A level topic chosen, the hypothesis chosen and the research method(s) adopted.

Student example ideas

Looking through this seven stage approach to the research process is aimed at helping to see the importance of these three elements being linked to form a coherent project. In addition to looking at an example in this way, it is also instructive at this point to introduce the three projects which will be regularly referred to in each chapter. Each is an actual project submitted for the AEB examination since the project option was established in 1991. Student A produced a high quality piece of work which gained a grade 'A', Student B gained a very creditable 'B' grade and the third example, Student C, only just gained a pass grade 'E'. The object of using extracts from each at various stages is to help differentiate good work from weaker work, and to enable learning from the recent experience of three differing candidates. At this juncture the hypothesis of each project is of greatest relevance, but that can be explored as part of a general summary of each of the three projects in the format of the idealised research procedure outlined directly above.

Student A: a project on education and gender

1 Observation

Student A had observed from her own experience of schooling that gender bias can occur in the classroom. As she clearly explains in the project's Rationale (or introductory statement of aims):

Sociologists such as Dale Spender, Michelle Stanworth and Katherine Clarricoates have all argued that within the classroom, teachers interact with, and give more attention to, male pupils/students as opposed to female pupils/students. Being in classrooms regularly myself I found their conclusions interesting and was intrigued to find out if such sex bias was occurring. Sociologists also claim that this sex bias during lessons reflects in females' attainment in both GCSE and A level results.

This succinctly sets the scene for the area of Student A's project and contains the link to an existing body of sociological work from which to develop an individual study. It illustrates how being interested in an area of a topic is a good basis from which to elaborate a hypothesis, as the student is genuinely seeking some researched answers to the question posed here.

2 Forming the hypothesis

The hypothesis was subsequently outlined in Student A's Rationale as follows:

I am therefore aiming to see if teachers interact more with male than female pupils/students and whether this influences differential academic attainment.

This hypothesis importantly contains the kind of theoretical link, or correlation, that was stated on page 22 as being essential to an A level project. This is because the A level project must address a theoretical aspect of the sociological area that a student chooses to research. The key part of the above hypothesis is the correlation made between levels of interaction by gender and levels of attainment by gender. Student A has made this explicit by saying 'and whether' at the linking part of the statement. Hence she is saying at the outset that her aim is to establish a causal relationship between the two variables of interaction and attainment. Not all hypotheses will be as definitely stated as this searched for causative link, but all must contain a theoretical angle that takes them beyond the merely descriptive. For example, if Student A had simply used the first half of the above statement only (before the 'and whether') she would have gained very few marks because to purely describe classroom interaction without the intention of explaining it, is insufficient for the board's requirements.

The remaining five stages are dealt with briefly here as their full content occurs later in the relevant section.

3 and 4 Choosing the method(s) and selecting the sample

Student A observed two secondary school classes and two college classes, with a male and a female teacher in each institution. She also distributed questionnaires to both pupils and teachers, and gathered secondary data on examination results by gender for the school, the college and nationally.

5 Gathering the data

Student A spent a number of weeks collecting both the primary and secondary data during the autumn and spring terms of her upper sixth year.

6 and 7 Analysing, concluding and considering policy implications

A strong feature of this project was the detailed and accurate evaluation of the findings, and relating them particularly to the overall sociological knowledge on gender bias in education. The policy problems were considered from the viewpoint of the long term and structural nature of the changes needed to achieve fairness (or equality) in schooling. The issue is one with many aspects in common with other areas of the female experience of life, not just those of education. Importantly, Student A rigorously related her findings to her opening hypothesis.

Student B: a project on aspects of the mother/ housewife role

1 Observation

From studying the topic of gender, Student B decided to further her understanding of changing conjugal roles (the roles that husband and wife or two partners adopt in relation to domestic labour and decision making). She is clear in her Rationale that her background reading on the subject of gender has informed her understanding of the dispute as to whether sex roles are biologically or ideologically constructed (most sociologists assert the latter), and that her aim is to see if the tasks done by both partners in the home are likely to become more equal.

As Student B writes in her Rationale:

The area of sociology I decided to study was the gender oriented issue of conjugal roles. I chose this area of sociology as it is one of the most debated subjects in sociology. I wished to find out how women viewed their roles within a family, anticipated and actual.

Hence the origin of her own interest and the debate within the discipline on conjugal roles are focused on when introducing the project and explaining its aims.

2 Forming the hypothesis

Having briefly discussed the disputed origin of sex roles, and briefly included some data on men generally doing less in the home, Student B outlines her hypothesis:

The anticipated experiences of unmarried women differ from those of married women in relation to the mother and housewife role.

The objective here is to compare married women's actual experience of conjugal roles with what those not yet married feel they would wish to have from their future relationship.

3 and 4 Choosing the method(s) and selecting the sample

Student B decided

to use the qualitative methods of unstructured and structured interviews, as I wanted to know what women experienced and how they felt about those experiences in the case of the married women, and for the unmarried I wished to determine what they expected to happen.

In justifying this choice of method, this student sensitively considers the less appropriate nature of other research techniques such as questionnaires, and the complete inapplicability in this context of more intrusive methods such as Participant Observation (how does the researcher unobtrusively gain access to a couple's relationship at their home?). The interviews were conducted in the women's homes and tape recorded for ease of data analysis later and so the student did not have to take notes during the interview. In further explaining her application of method, Student B writes:

All the interviews lasted from one to two and a half hours long. The interviews were taped and the information on these tapes was placed under general headings by myself, and then later analysed and compared to findings in my context and to other research. However this could be interpreted differently by different people. The evidence can be viewed in many ways, and is subjective to my knowledge of the subject.

Here she is demonstrating an awareness of possible methodological bias entering into the data analysis, as it will be her interpretations of the interview materials that form the answer to the hypothesis posed. All researchers face this dilemma, some more equably than others. It has been a facet of much phenomenologically styled Participant Observation work to simply acknowledge such bias may exist and let the reader make their own allowances: Howard Becker did this in his famous study of drug-using musician groups *Outsiders* (Becker, 1963). In the case of Student B she has correctly raised the point to qualify the conclusions she, and the reader draw from her study.

5 Gathering the data

In this instance, the need (for the type of qualitative hypothesis posed) to gain large amounts of in-depth data on experiences and feelings meant Student B spent a considerable amount of time conducting a total of twenty interviews, the minimum length of which was one hour (see above). Obtaining the right kind of interviewees also involved careful thought and planning, as Student B explains in her Methodology section:

My sample consisted of ten married women, and ten unmarried women, who were obtained through stratified sampling. The total sample's ages ranged from 16 to 26, as beyond this age bracket it may have been difficult to find never married single women. Also older women's views and attitudes would vary from the younger samples due to changing cultural attitudes. As my hypothesis also concerns the mother role, my married sample needed to have some experience of looking after a child.

This illustrates a careful attention to the appropriateness of the methodology to the chosen hypothesis.

6 and 7 Analysing, concluding and considering policy implications

The presentation of a large amount of qualitative prose data was done well in this project, as Student B divided the material into three differing formats:

- A brief individual profile of each woman.
- Subject headings for analysis of certain themes; for example, data collected and analysed under the themes of 'housework' and 'childcare' from across the sample.
- Brief summaries in table form of who most often performed various domestic tasks.

In concluding, Student B was (to her detriment) somewhat briefer than Student A but nevertheless evaluated her main findings accurately and with reference to existing sociological knowledge and her opening aims/hypothesis. She did not, however, consider any policy implications which again slightly detracts from her ending Evaluation section. There are many possibilities that could be summarised relevantly: from greater workplace based availability of childbirth to enable young women to remain in work after child-care and hence have less of an 'automatic' caring home role, to how our society could more positively picture males in domestic environments (although this is admittedly not a direct function of government in the strict sense of policy outlined earlier).

Student C: a study on education and gender

1 Observation

In common with Student A's project, this one also investigated the issue of differential gender attainment in the classroom, although Student C did so in the context of primary age schooling and also to less high a standard than Student A.

In a much too brief Rationale of two paragraphs, Student C outlines an interest in her chosen area of study and refers to the work of Katherine Clarricoates in observing the gender behaviours of young children in primary schools. By being so brief, however, Student C has not comprehensively set out the reason for the study, which is the purpose of the Rationale.

2 Forming the hypothesis

This is stated as:

Does any gender stereotyping by primary school teachers affect pupil behaviour or aspiration?

This hypothesis actually requires slight re-phrasing to be a testable proposition rather than a question; consider how this could be done before reading on.
   Two sample alternatives could be as follows:

(i)   Gender stereotyping of pupils by primary school teachers affects pupil behaviour and aspiration.
(ii) There is gender stereotyping present in primary school classrooms which affects how pupils behave and/or their aspirations.

Both these suggestions are statements rather than questions.

3 and 4 Choosing the method(s) and selecting the sample

Student C's Methodology section is again rather brief and does not sufficiently justify the choice of methods to gain high rewards from the mark scheme (this will be explored in more detail in the section on the Methodology p. 49). Two methods were employed: a non-participant observation and a questionnaire with the teacher of the class observed. These are certainly not inappropriate methods, but their selection did need justification and there was an additional problem with the sample base as only one class was observed. Clearly this is highly particularised data (particular to that one observed class), even given the restrictions imposed by being a solitary A level student.

5 Gathering the data

This was all conducted on one morning's visit to the chosen school lasting two or three hours. Data was collected from one class only. The class teacher filled in the questionnaire, but Student C did not communicate with any other teachers in this school or any other local schools.

6 and 7 Analysing, concluding and considering policy implications

Although Student C submitted full length Evaluation and Results sections, they were simplistic and lacked reference to other sociological findings. Unsupported statements such as

It has been said by certain sociologists that children can be pushed towards certain subjects by their teachers

are not acceptable. It must be stated which sociologists are being referred to specifically, otherwise the examiner will conclude (probably correctly) that the candidate has not made the effort to locate the evaluative discussion within a context of existing sociological work. Broader implications of the student's findings and/or policy issues were unfortunately entirely lacking.
   Before concluding this important opening section on finding a hypothesis, complete the exercise below:

Exercise on Student A B C Hypotheses

Looking again particularly at the hypotheses of Students A and B, write short paragraph answers to the two questions below and then compare them to the answers presented in Chapter 6, p. 115.

(i) What difficulties might be anticipated for the hypotheses of Students A and B? (Student C's hypothesis has been scrutinised above).

(ii) Looking especially at stages 1 to 4 of the research process for Students A, B and C, do any aspects of the research seem poorly integrated? For example, is a very qualitative type of hypothesis then followed by quantitative methods, or is the hypothesis – theory – method balance a well-integrated one?

Hypothesis Checklist

Before moving on, check your hypothesis generated from the earlier exercise against the following:

● Is the hypothesis a statement rather than a question?

● Does it relate to a part of the A level Sociology syllabus?

● Is it specific about an area of work and/or an issue that can be tested?

● Could it be proved right or wrong by the subsequent research?

● Is it testable in a legal and ethical manner?

● Does it contain a theoretical aspect to be tested? (to merely describe part of the social world is not sufficient)

● Does it contain consistent and accurate use of ordinary and sociological terminology?

If the answer to any of these checklist points is no, it would be advisable to re-think and/or consult a course tutor before continuing.

*T*HE *R*ATIONALE AND THE *C*ONTEXT

These are actually two separate sections that will form the first and second parts of the written up project (see Chapter 1 for the overall outline of the project). They are dealt with together in this chapter, as the Rationale and Context form the explanation of why the project is being done and what body of sociological work it forms a part of.

Definitions

The Rationale is thus the (relatively brief) opening section of the project. Here the preliminary observations that led to the choice of study are explained, along with the aims of the enquiry and a statement of the hypothesis. It is also common good practice to include a comment or two on the possible outcome of the research, along the lines of what might be expected to be discovered.

The Context is the longer, following section which should be a well-researched discussion of the sociological issues and previous sociological work that surrounds the chosen topic for the project. This is not a general 'essay' on, for example, education if that is the topic area, but must be a body of selected material that relates specifically to the chosen hypothesis, and is presented in relation to it.

These points for both the Rationale and the Context are sufficiently important to need reinforcement in the exercises which follow, as students often have some difficulties defining what needs to be included in these two sections and also *how* the written material should be focused.

The Rationale

The key way of understanding what form and content the Rationale must take is to apply the mark scheme from the Associated Examining Board to sample Rationales. Rather than present the entire mark scheme here (it is three pages long and has numerous sections) we reproduce below the section that relates directly to the Rationale. It should be pointed out that the Rationale is marked under what is termed the Interpretation and Application section, which assesses the ability of the candidate to apply selected sociological information to an issue and correctly interpret the implications of what is learnt. The overall mark scheme assesses three 'skill domains'.

1 Knowledge and Understanding: the ability to make accurate sense of and correctly include sociological information. This skill accounts for 26% of the total marks, covering in particular the Context and Methodology sections of the final written project.

2 Interpretation and Application: as defined above, is the candidate's ability to correctly apply and analyse sociological information. This skill accounts for 37% of the total marks, covering in particular the Rationale and the results

(which the Board calls the Content) sections, but also covering how applicable the chosen methodology is for the stated hypothesis.

3 Evaluation: the skill of assessing evidence gained from the study. This is where good written discussion skills can be highly rewarded, as this skill domain accounts for the remaining 37% of the marks. It covers in particular the actual section at the end of the project called the Evaluation, and also (again, as for 2) aspects of the Methodology – is the chosen methodology justified for its use and is it assessed for its weaknesses?

As an aside here (the point is further explored in Chapter 4), it should be noted from the above summary that the Methodology section is included in all three skill domains. This clearly implies that stronger candidates will have carefully selected, justified and sensitively applied the chosen methodology, as well as showing competent understanding of it. Another point to stress is that knowledge and understanding alone (presentation of facts and correct including of material) is actually a fairly small part of the overall mark scheme. Although it is obviously important, the bulk of the marks are attached to the skills of analysis.

Reproduced below in table 2 is the section of the Associated Examining Board mark scheme which covers the Rationale:

Mark	Rationale for study (hypothesis/aims/preliminary observations)
0	No interpretation or application.
1 – 4	A minimal statement of the Rationale is included.
5 – 8	An appropriate Rationale is included but the study does not relate closely to it.
9 – 12	An appropriate and reasonably comprehensive Rationale is included and the study (including its conclusions) relates to it.
13 – 17	An appropriate and comprehensive Rationale is included and the study (and its conclusions) explicitly relates to it.

Table 2

What the marking Tutor does is firstly decide which broad points range the candidate's Rationale fits into, and then further decide which actual mark in that range it has achieved. The descriptions written beside the mark ranges are to assist in this process. It should be clear from the comments next to each mark range above that the mark scheme applies across the whole project. In other words, in marking the Rationale, the marker must consider how integrated it is with the rest of the project, and in particular with the conclusions. Assume for the exercise immediately below that both students' researches did relate to the Rationale, although one did so more than the other. (Marks and comments are in Chapter 6, p. 118.)

Rationale exercise

Below are two sample Rationales from the projects selected for use throughout these exercises. Read them carefully and then decide:

- What mark to give them.
- What is required for each to be a full and comprehensive Rationale.

Rationale from Student B

The area of sociology I decided to study was the gender oriented issue of conjugal roles. I chose this area of sociology as it is one of the most debated subjects in sociology. I wished to find out how women viewed their roles within a family, anticipated and actual.

For some sociologists traditional roles are biologically determined. Theorists Tiger and Fox in The Imperial Animal, *1972 state that men are naturally stronger and assertive; women, however, are weaker than men, and are naturally dependent and passive. Evidence such as this would perhaps suggest that the female gender role should be the same throughout the world. However, this is not so, as not all societies regard women as weaker than men.*

Another theory, that of radical feminism, suggests that women's position in the family benefits patriarchy and capital. Hartman, in Capitalism, Patriarchy and Job Segregation by Sex, *says women provide a market place for the products of capitalism and 'renew' the workforce.*

Both these ways would seem to suggest that gender roles are not easily changeable; the former due to biology, the latter due to ideology. Yet Willmott and Young believe that conjugal roles are changing. After their study at Bethnal Green they concluded that families were becoming more symmetrical. The family was changing and becoming more 'home-centred'. From this evidence one may conclude that younger women would not be so willing to conform to the traditional mother and housewife role, if the symmetrical family exists.

Nonetheless, most men occasionally or never perform the tasks of cleaning, shopping, cooking, washing-up or gardening, even when their wife worked and 90% had dependent children (the Equal Opportunities Research, funded by the Equal Opportunities Commission and SSRC, 1981).

From this evidence, I derived my hypothesis:
'The anticipated experiences of unmarried women differ from those of married women in relation to the housewife and mother role.'

I decided to use the qualitative methods of unstructured and structured interviews, as I wanted to know what women experienced and how they felt about these experiences in the case of the married women, and for the unmarried women I wished to determine what they expected to happen. My total sample of twenty women may not have been very large or wholly representative, but I hoped the information would be lengthy and detailed, so as to complete a study on conjugal roles, their effects on women and their beliefs and attitudes towards the gender role they occupy.

Rationale from Student C

It has been argued that teachers sometimes treat pupils differently depending on their sex, to affect the way in which they act both inside the classroom and in the playground. This has been especially noticeable within the younger years of primary school. I found this very interesting and decided to investigate it further to see if points which have been made by sociologists such as Spender and Clarricoates were true. For example, Clarricoates discovered in her observation of primary schools the way in which boys are discouraged from behaving in 'cissy' ways, whereas girls are discouraged from being 'tomboys'. She also noticed that when playing, girls played games such as housekeeping, while boys who played in the Wendy House risked the teacher's disapproval. Another example is that given by Spender where she indicates that girls are often rendered 'invisible' through lack of attention and recognition.

In order to see if these points were true, I set a hypothesis which was 'Does any gender stereotyping by primary school teachers affect pupil behaviour or aspiration?'. I decided that the best way to approach it would be to go into a school and observe a class to see if the teacher was making any stereotypings amongst the children, and then to ask the children themselves a few questions. Lastly, I decided on either an interview or questionnaire for the teacher of the class which I observed.

The Context (with exemplars)

This section of the project is dealt with in two stages below. First, the question of how the Context should be focused and structured as a scholarly written piece is addressed. Secondly, the Context is considered as a process: how to gather materials of all kinds that are relevant to the chosen research area and how to direct background reading so that it is purposeful and appropriate.

In a sociology essay, it may occasionally be necessary to set ideas in a context. For example, when evaluating the functionalist explanation of deviance of Robert Merton, it is helpful and good practice to briefly set this in the context of functionalism as a general theory of society. It would briefly be made clear in a good student essay that functionalism's tendency as an overall theory to stress shared social goals and norms forms the basis of Merton's goals/means analysis of criminal, or what he calls non-conformist, behaviour (for an outline of Merton on deviance see p. 323 in Mike O'Donnell's *Introduction to Sociology*, 3rd Edition). The Context of the project is very similar to this, in that it should enable someone less familiar with the chosen area than the researcher to understand the main issues surrounding the current enquiry. It serves, then, to inform of other, already existing sociological work in the domain of the problematic or hypothesis which is being investigated.

Set out below are edited extracts from a Context (written by Student C). This will repay a close, full reading before going any further with work on the background to the Context. It is a valuable exercise to work backwards from a completed Context to consider and learn how best to approach the secondary sources reading and writing stage of a research enquiry. Footnotes are added to the text of Student C's Context so as to build up a picture of its efficacy, and to guide the current reader's thoughts on ways of approaching this task.

Context from Student C's project (an enquiry into gender stereotyping in a primary school)

There have been many sociologists who have studied gender and education together in a number of cases, some of these being Dale Spender, Christine Griffin, Katherine Clarricoates and Delamont. Each of these has significant links with my hypothesis of 'Does any gender stereotyping occur amongst primary school teachers to affect pupils' behaviour or aspiration?'.

Firstly, there is Dale Spender's study on Invisible Woman: The Schooling Scandal. *In this, she says that women are inferior and wrong and therefore do not deserve the same consideration as men. The same process continues today in most of the classrooms of this country where, in mixed set classes, males are the authority figures as they do most of the talking out in the lessons. The lessons are designed to cater for male interests because it is thought that if they are not then the males will get bored and try and cause trouble to amuse themselves. At this moment, female students are being dismissed and the experience of women is no more likely to be the substance of the curriculum in a mixed sex school, than the experience of women has been the substance of our social knowledge.*

She goes on to say that it is often said that the teachers are unaware of the unfair attention they pay towards the boys and when asked, they protest that they treat each sex equally. But when their next lesson is taped, it is often found that over two-thirds of their time was given to the boys who comprised less than half of the class. A majority of teachers say that they want to treat the sexes fairly and not discriminate against girls, but our society and education are so structured that 'fairness' and 'equality' mean that males get more attention.

Dale Spender points out that from the perspective of female and male structures it is felt by the teachers that the boys are seen as more important, more in charge, more deserving and worthy of attention, and as the students know this, it leads to making the boys more confident and the girls lose their confidence.

Comments

This is a good, clear beginning in which Student C refers to her problematic / hypothesis and begins to explore the work of one prominent researcher in this field. There is an unfortunate inaccuracy at point (1), in that this sentence implies Spender has a denigrating view of female potential. Spender actually stresses exactly the opposite in her book *Invisible Woman*, and is adamant in her view that women suffer from just such condescending misperceptions as these and should strive to correct them. This sentence may be the result of a misunderstanding by Student C or poor phrasing, but is misleading and inaccurate nonetheless.

Another problem then becomes evident as Student C continues after this point with a further page and a half on Spender's work, describing her findings in great, unanalysed detail. It is sufficient to make the point, without including this section of her Context here, that over-reliance on one or two sources of reference only, is indicative of poor background research skills or paucity of effort.

Student C then continues:

Spender's study also shows that Katherine Clarricoates (1978) interviewed a number of primary school teachers and each of them provided clear evidence that they geared their classes towards the interests of boys as that was the only way the class could be controlled.

Angela Parker (1973) questioned students; both sexes stated that asking questions, challenging the authority of teachers, demanding reasons and explanations was a masculine activity.

She pointed out that all these were acts of the classroom, so is therefore implying that females do not become involved in these activities. Both sexes know that girls who do not conform to these expectations are likely to be punished.

Spender points out that when boys ask questions, protest, or challenge the teacher they are often met with rewards and respect. When girls take part in exactly the same actions they are often met with punishment and rebuke. The girls in this situation would be labelled unladylike! It is expected that boys should stand up for themselves, even if and when this may be inconvenient for a teacher, it is behaviour from boys that is still likely to be viewed positively. It is not expected that girls should act in an independent manner, and if they do, their behaviour is frequently seen as inappropriate, viewed negatively, and in many cases is classified as a 'problem'. Teachers can continue to treat their students in this sexually differentiated way because in our society males are perceived as more important. In a society where it is normal for males to receive preferential treatment, it is also normal to provide such preferential treatment in school.

Katherine Clarricoates completed a study titled The Importance of Being Earnest...Emma...Tom...Jane. In it she constructs masculinity and femininity within primary schools. She observed four different types of school which were a traditional working class school, a modern suburban middle class school, a council estate school and lastly a very small rural primary school. From all her observations she noticed that the classrooms were arranged either as informal workshops or pedagogic 'absorption tanks'. She also says that masculine and feminine are based on ecological factors which pertain to that school.

Comments

There is an immediate and a more structural problem with the approach Student C is now taking. On an immediate level, sociological concepts obtained from a reading of a study are included here without any attempt to define them, or explain their relevance to the student's research. Not all sociologists would be able to explain what a 'pedagogic absorption tank' is, and the idea that 'ecological factors affect masculinity and femininity also needs fully explaining. Instead, it is apparent that Student C has not understood these concepts but has included them anyway as they sound quite impressive. If in doubt at any point when reading background material, it is advisable to ask as to its relevance from a tutor.

The more structural problem is slightly more complicated. Just as it seems as if the student has completed the work on Spender, and has moved on to other issues or information with Parker, the text darts back to Spender before going on to Clarricoates. There is a need for a tight structure to this kind of writing, with a discipline imposed from a pre-planned format. As in the essay work of Sociology courses, it is possible to structure written work of this academic kind in two broad ways.

1 Structure by putting information into 'chunks' ('chunking', in the jargon) : this means the writing falls into areas of separable work, with each explained as having its particular relevance to the problematic or hypothesis at hand. This might mean, in the instance of this study dealing with the work of several researchers on the issue of differential educational attainment by gender in one or two paragraph chunks, always regularly synthesising points so as to relate to the issue of the problem under study.

Student C has attempted this strategy in her Context, but has:

- not researched into sufficient materials, so two or three studies are heavily over-relied on
- not kept to a reasonably tight chunking format, and instead strays from points and begins paragraphs sometimes without reference to what has previously been written.

2 Structure by using themes to the sociological material: this means the major themes relating to the problematic or hypothesis are identified beforehand, and each one is explored in two or three paragraphs. Such an approach needs careful ordering of the themes before writing, and works differently to the method suggested above because the work of several sociologists and the thoughts of the writer her/himself – are grouped around one issue at a time, for example:

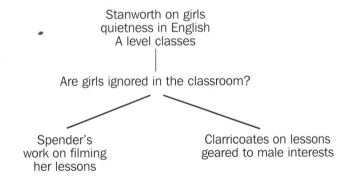

Developing this theme of one gender getting more attention than another in the classroom would, then, involve exploring that specific aspect of the work of researchers such as those mentioned above, so as to:

(i) draw out similarities and differences between their findings
(ii) relate their findings to the point at issue in the student's inquiry.

This could then be followed by exploring another chosen aspect of the gender differentiation topic, such as:

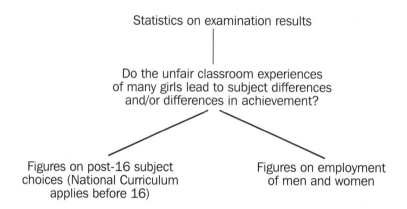

Statistics on examination results

Do the unfair classroom experiences of many girls lead to subject differences and/or differences in achievement?

Figures on post-16 subject choices (National Curriculum applies before 16)

Figures on employment of men and women

In this theme, the effects of any substantiated gender inequalities in the classroom are explored with a view to their longer lasting impact on the lives of men and women (and the evidence certainly suggests there is a lasting and generally discriminating effect for many females).

By adopting this structuring strategy the student can organise and synthesise material around the central issue. Although more complex than the first method suggested above, this latter approach can be highly rewarding in terms of innovative, imaginative writing. For further reading on the researchers and issues mentioned in these two examples, see:

- Spender pp. 154–61 in O'Donnell's *Reader in Sociology*, 2nd Edition is an excellent extract, which also touches on Stanworth and Clarricoates' work.
- Stanworth pp. 65–6 in *Sociology in Focus*: Education, by Stephen Ball.
- General material on statistical trends of which there there is a very helpful and up-to-date section on gender and education in O'Donnell's *Introduction to Sociology*, 3rd Edition, pp. 96 –101.

Student C then continues with the work of Clarricoates in considerable detail for another full page before finishing as below:

Another example of stereotyping in her study can be shown in the line of punishment. For example girls are never known to get the slipper whereas if boys do something wrong that is serious then they automatically go to the Head to get the slipper. But the boys seem to like this form of punishment as they can brag about the amount of times they have had the slipper and they feel it is a sign of being tough.

Christine Griffin took part in a study titled 'Its different for girls'.

Comments

This is a strangely abrupt ending which detracts from this Context. It would be expected to continue to explore the (relevant) research of Griffin into gender experiences of working class girls in the classroom and at work, but instead Student C has abruptly finished. What is needed is a measured and thoughtful, brief summing up of the main work or themes developed over the preceding pages, with a final point on how this sociological background informs the student's current project. This need only be ten to fifteen lines in length, but avoids the 'hanging in air' aspect seen with this example.

Overall, although Student C has produced a written body of work of some relevance to her task, it is poorly synthesised and inadequately organised.

Some of the learning to be derived from sifting through key elements of a context are summarised in the checklist at the end of this chapter.

Researching Background Information

Moving from a general, or even specific idea for a research enquiry to locating relevant background information, is a vital stage in the process of a social investigation. What sort of information is required to place the particular research idea in its sociological context? Where can such information be gathered? These are two central questions that must be addressed before undertaking any actual reading.

With most project areas, a number of types of information can usually be gathered:

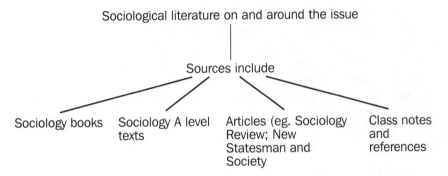

Sociological literature on and around the issue

Sources include

Sociology books — Sociology A level texts — Articles (eg. Sociology Review; New Statesman and Society) — Class notes and references

Remember it is important to *target* this information when gathering it so that it has fairly direct relevance to the chosen topic area; it is *not any* information on education and gender that will be helpful to a project in that area, as it will depend what the study is specifically on as to which particular bits of data are relevant. For example:

- If studying differential attainment, examination results and career aspirations are keys areas.
- If studying negative teacher stereotypes of female ability, the literature on observations of the classroom for gender bias is relevant (as in Student C's enquiry examined above, although her background work was across too narrow a spectrum of studies).
- If studying the education system as a major reinforcer and enhancer of gender differences (masculinity versus femininity) in children, the work of educationalists and sociologists on secondary socialisation (that stage of learning our culture that takes place outside the home) is the prime background research concern.

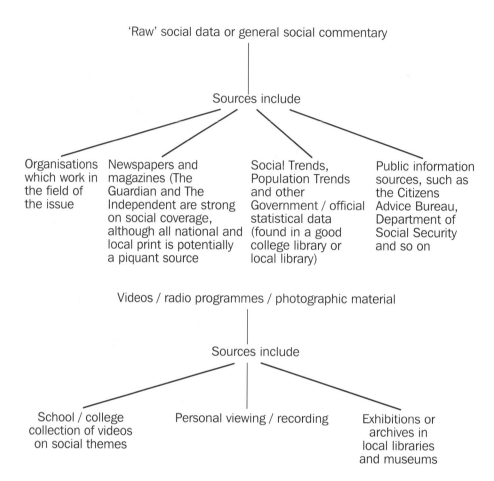

'Raw' social data or general social commentary

Sources include

| Organisations which work in the field of the issue | Newspapers and magazines (The Guardian and The Independent are strong on social coverage, although all national and local print is potentially a piquant source | Social Trends, Population Trends and other Government / official statistical data (found in a good college library or local library) | Public information sources, such as the Citizens Advice Bureau, Department of Social Security and so on |

Videos / radio programmes / photographic material

Sources include

| School / college collection of videos on social themes | Personal viewing / recording | Exhibitions or archives in local libraries and museums |

These electronic or visual forms of social information are very useful in gaining ideas, and can often contain excellent, up-to-date data as well as interviews with people at the centre of a particular social issue / problem. Their actual application to the written format of the project requires that these sources of information are noted from, so as to become textual in nature. Hence, noting the words of a part of an interview with the Government Minister for Housing may be very relevant to the background data of a student enquiry on homelessness or poverty.

Many programmes on television and radio explore social issues. Apart from news programmes (which should be regularly watched in any case), documentaries and one-off investigative programmes can be a rich source of contemporary commentary. In recent years many sociological problems have been brought to a wider public in this way, from racism (two journalists, one black and one white, applying for flats and bed-and-breakfasts using a concealed video camera) to homelessness (a young reporter went 'native', in the mode of a covert participant observation study in London for a month, living on the streets and begging for food while a cameraman filmed secretly from a distance).

Organisations That Can be Contacted

One valuable source of additional information for the project overall, but especially for the Context section, are the multitude of individual organisations that exist to support particular causes. These can provide well-researched and up-to-date information on aspects of a chosen project area, as well as stimulating further thought on, for example, exactly which questions to ask in the research-gathering stage itself.

Follow the procedure below when contacting any such organisations for information:

- Make sure the broad project area is already firmly established before writing; a random scatter contacting of lots of organisations will only be expensive and time-consuming.
- Write a brief, polite and clear letter requesting specific information and (if possible) say what the chosen project is about.
- Include some contribution to return postage.
- Write early on in the project timescale – in the middle summer of the A level course or the second year autumn term. Replies can often take some time.

The organisations below are not to be seen as an exhaustive list, and it may be that others are known or suggested to students as the project progresses. The more widely sources are consulted, the more accurately and interestingly informed the final project will be.

Organisations (grouped under broader sociological interest areas):

Health / Illness

Action for Disability, 19/27 Young Street, Kensington, London W8.
Action on Addiction, York House, 199 Westminster Bridge Road, London SE1.
Action on Smoking and Health (ASH), 109 Gloucester Place, London W1H.
Alcohol Concern, 275 Grays Inn Road, London WC1X.
British Diabetic Association, 10 Queen Anne Street, London W1.
Disabled Living Foundation, 380/384 Harrow Road, London W9.
Foundation for the Study of Infant Deaths, 35 Belgrave Square, London SW1X.
General Welfare of the Blind, 37/55 Ashburton Grove,London N7.
Institute for the Study of Drugs Dependence, 1 Hatton Place, London EC1.
National Aids Trust, 14th Floor, Euston Tower, 286 Euston Road, London.
Royal National Institute for the Blind, 224 Great Portland Street, London W1N 6AA.

Deviance / Criminality

Ealing Drug Advisory Service, 14 Alexandria Road, Ealing W5.
Legal Action For Women, c/o Kings Cross Women's Centre, 71 Tonbridge Street, London WC1H.

National Association for the Care and Resettlement of Offenders (NACRO)
National Council for Civil Liberties, 21 Tabard Street, London SE1.
Prisoners Wives and Families Society, 254 Caledonian Road, London N1.
Police Complaints Authority, 10 Great George Street, London SW1P.
The Samaritans, 106 Felsham Road, Putney, London SW15.

The Media

Advertising Standards Authority, Brook House, 2–16 Torrington Place, London WC1E 7HN.
British Broadcasting Corporation (BBC), Broadcasting House, Portland Place, London W1A.
British Film Institute, BFI Publications, 81 Dean Street, London W1V 6AA.
Broadcasting Complaints Commission, Grosvenor Gardens House, 35 & 37 Grosvenor Gardens, London SW1W.
Broadcasting Standards Council (BSC), 5 / 8 The Sanctuary, London SW1P.
Campaign for Freedom of Information, 88 Old Street, London EC1V.
Campaign for Press and Broadcasting Freedom, 9 Poland Street, London W1V 3DG.
Channel 4 TV Co. Ltd., 60 Charlotte Street, London W1P.
Independent Television Commission (ITC), 70 Brompton Road, London SW3.
Press Complaints Commission, 1 Salisbury Square, London EC4Y.

Education

Department For Education, Elizabeth House, York Road, London SE1.
Independent Schools Information Service (ISIS), 56 Buckingham Gate,London SW1E.
National Council for Vocational Qualifications, 222 Euston Road, London NW1.
National Foundation for Educational Research , Darville House, 2 Oxford Road, Windsor, Berkshire, Sl4 1DF.

Age

Age Concern, 19–27 Young Street, London W8.
Barnardo's, 4 Ferncliff Road, London E8.
Centre for Policy on Ageing, 25–31 Ironmonger Row, London EC1V.
Child 2000, 33 Pancras Road, NW1.
Child Poverty Action Group, 1–5 Bath Street, London EC1V.
Childline, Studd Street, London N1.
Cruse – Bereavement Care, Cruse House, 126 Sheen Road, Richmond, Surrey TW9.
Foundation for the Study of Infant Deaths, 35 Belgrave Square, London SW1X.
Help the Aged, St James Walk, London EC1R OVE.
National Childrens' Bureau, 8 Wakley Street, London EC1V.
National Society for the Prevention of Cruelty to Children (NSPCC), 16–18 Hatton Garden, London EC1N.
Research Into Ageing, 49 Queen Victoria Street, EC4N.

Family

Exploring Parenthood, Latimer Education Centre, 194 Freston Road, London W10.
Family Mediators Association, 14 Weston Park, Thames Ditton, Surrey KT7.

Family Rights Group, The Prince House, 18 Ashwin Street, London E8.
Family Welfare Association, 202 Upper Street, London N1.
Gingerbread (support group for one-parent families) 35 Wellington Street, London WC2E.
Institute of Family Therapy, 43 New Cavendish Street, London W1M.
International Planned Parenthood Federation, Regents College, Inner Circle, Regents Park, London NW1.
Relate, Marriage Guidance, 30 Worple Road, London SW19.

Gender

African Women's Support Group, Southwark Training Centre, Copperfield Street, London SE1.
Backup Domestic Violence Support Group, PO Box 483, 44 Nelson Square, SE1.
Equal Opportunities Commission, 52 Poland Street, London W1V.
Gay Bereavement Project Helpline, Vaughan Williams Centre, Collingdale Hospital, London NW9.
The Lesbian Archive and Information Centre: phone 071 405 6475.
The London Institute of Human Sexuality, 10 Warwick Road, Earls Court Square, London SW5.
National Abortion Campaign, Wesley House, 4 Wild Court, London WC2B.
Post Abortion Counselling Service, 340 Westbourne Park Road, London W11.
Welsh Women's Aid, 38 / 42 Crwys Road, Cardiff, Wales.
Women and Development Programme, Human Resource Development Group, Commonwealth Secretariat, Marlborough House, Pall Mall, London SW1 5HX.

Homelessness / Poverty

Advisory Service for Squatters, 2 St Paul's Road, London N1.
Centrepoint Soho (a hostel for the homeless) Delancey House, 72 Delancey Street, London NW1.
Hostel Vacancy Project, 189a Old Brompton Road, London SW5.
Housing Choice, 56 Britton Street, London EC1M.
Kings Cross Homelessness Project, Gregory House, 48 Mecklenburgh Square, London WC1N.
Shelter, National Campaign for the Homeless Ltd., 88 Old Street, London EC1V.
(also try contacting the local housing department for the area in which you live.)

Ethnicity

African Welfare and Resource Centre, Unit 21, Bridge Park, Brentfield Harrow Road, London NW10.
Commission for Racial Equality, Elliott House, 10 - 12 Allington Street, London SW1E.
Immigration Law Practitioners Association (ILPA), 115 Old Street, London EC1V.
National Ethic Minority Advisory Council, Brent Employment Training Workshop, Park Mews Estate, Cambridge Road, Kilburn, London NW6.
United Kingdom Immigrants Advisory Service, Room 0001a, Queens Building, Heathrow Airport, Hounslow TW6.

General

Central Statistical Office, Government Offices, Great George Street, London SWIP 3AQ.
Citizens Advice Bureau, Alhambra House, 33 Charing Cross Road, London WC2H.
Members of Parliament (any), House of Commons, London SW1A.
Low Pay Unit, 27–29 Amwell Street, London EC1R 1UN.
(any) Trades Union Congress, Great Russell Street, London WC1B.

Checklist for the Context

- Make sure the information gathered is from a wide range of sources and includes some contemporary (up-to-date) information particularly; do not over rely on sociology books which are well past their sell by date.
- Have a test for the relevance of the gathered data:
  - how does it inform the project's chosen subject of study?
  - how does it compare with the anticipated findings of the project?

Asking these two questions of all the information gathered should help weed out what is tangential and highlight what is central.

- Include material that is preferably in some differing formats. For example, consider if there is any statistical data that might inform the problem under investigation, or if any visual presentations are applicable (although do not feel a purely prose context is inappropriate).

- Refer to the hypothesis or problematic at issue at key points, emphasising the material's relationship with it and how the material informs the investigation.

- As in an essay, assume the reader is not familiar with concepts and terms pertaining to the chosen area of study, and explain them briefly as they are used.

- In summarising, return to the issue at the centre of the enquiry and re-state the direction of existing sociological data on the issue.

- When gathering material for this background work (which will take several weeks, often a couple of months) keep a running list of sources being used to compile a bibliography in the following standard academic format:

  Author's surname, initials. Book/article title, publisher, city of publication, date.

  For example:

  Pahl, R. Divisions of Labour,Blackwell, Oxford, 1984.

  Or, where there is more than one author, they appear alphabetically by surname:

  Crompter, R., Jones, G. White-Collar Proletariat, Deskilling and Gender in Clerical Work, Macmillan, London, 1984.

CHAPTER 4

CONDUCTING THE RESEARCH

Before reaching this stage in an enquiry, the researcher will have spent a lot of time considering the area of enquiry, the nature of the problem under consideration and the sociological literature that already informs the issue. Hence, before conducting the research, much work has already been done to direct and order the process it could take. There are essentially three stages to this research process:

1   Planning the research.
2   Conducting it (gathering the data).
3   Interpreting the data and writing up results.

This section will cover the first two of these main elements by containing the following:

- A review of the methods available to a researcher.
- Examples of one or two sociological studies under each method that a student could refer to. There are also either suggested texts and page numbers as follow up references, or the book titles themselves.
- An example study on combining methods.
- A section on sampling techniques; defining them briefly and assigning them to types of study (qualitative / quantitative and by method(s) used).
- Advice on designing the methodology; ie: having chosen the method, what questions will be asked, and so on. This includes the use of pilot studies in a final checklist for the research process overall.

The following chapter looks at the practical aspects of methodology such as presentation. This includes student examples of methods in action and how best to present results.

Methods Available to the Researcher

A preliminary distinction to make when considering how research methods differ is between primary and secondary sources.

Primary sources of data involve the gathering and generation of original data by the sociologist as s/he conducts the enquiry. Hence this is fresh, new information pertaining to the issue or area being studied. Secondary sources of data are those which either already exist in the form of past research done by others, or are generated by other social agencies such as in government official statistics, academic articles, archives, newspapers, television and so on.

Clearly then, a distinction must be made between methods which enable the generation of primary data, and those sources which are characterised as secondary data. In summary form, this can be shown in table 3.

Primary sources		Secondary sources
Participant observation and non-participant observation (PO / non-PO) Structured / focused / unstructured interviews	Using a combination of primary and secondary sources (known as triangulation)	Official statistics Historical materials The media Documentary sources
Questionnaires Documents of life (or the life history method) and diaries Content analysis Case studies (social experiments, social surveys and conversation analysis are also briefly explored).		

Table 3

It is possible to produce a research enquiry using purely primary data in the research gathering process, or indeed it is equally possible to not originate any data and pursue an issue purely through studying and analysing secondary sources of data. The latter course of action can be quite demanding in that the student needs to be very confident at the outset that sufficient sources and content of information exist for a viable enquiry. Nevertheless, this can be a successful and sociologically informative route to adopt. As an example, one highly rigorous student inquiry investigated experiences of becoming homeless to ascertain the main causes of, and consequences for the individuals concerned of, becoming homeless. It was rapidly apparent that the generation of primary data of a qualitative kind on this issue (qualitative data being preferable so as to capture the social experience of homelessness at the personal level) was going to be problematic because:

- Finding a sample of the homeless would be difficult: enquiries to the local council housing department revealed great reluctance, for reasons of confidentiality, to provide names and addresses of people temporarily homed in Bed and Breakfasts or other temporary accommodation.
- Even if such a list of potential respondents could be obtained, the individuals may not wish to answer a questionnaire or interview schedule with an unknown visitor, on a potentially embarrassing and personal issue.

What the student was able to negotiate with the local housing department, was to have photocopies of around thirty case studies that had had the names removed. These proved an excellent basis for an analysis of the causes and effects of local homelessness, although other secondary sources such as sociological studies of poverty and newspaper items were also relevantly included.

It is also often a fertile development to combine primary and secondary sources. Perhaps it would be as well to stress a small defining point here: all student enquiries will make *some* reference to secondary sources in that *they* will contain an evaluation of existing relevant sociological material (see the previous chapter). In particular cases, it may then be appropriate to make further substantial use of secondary sources to investigate specifically the problematic or hypothesis at issue. This is the combination referred to when stating the often fertile results from combining primary and secondary sources. In such an instance, a student may gather some data through one or more of the primary techniques above, and supplement the findings with secondary material.

To research purely along primary sourcing lines is arguably the most frequent student choice, and is nonetheless appropriate and productive. Many students do find that the most rewarding and engaging method is the primary one and successfully pursue it. What is perhaps central in this set of choices is the *appropriacy* of any particular chosen method(s). One of the intellectually flexible developments within sociology as a discipline in the 1980s was the tendency to move away from rigidity of the perspective – problem / issue – method equation. Thinkers such as, among others, Giddens, have stressed the concept of triangulation, or combining methods.

This has considerably freed-up the diversity of mix available to the sociological researcher (for an accessible, brief example of this style of work see Giddens, A. *Sociology*, Polity Press, Cambridge, 1989, pp. 682–4). It is possible to use combinations of primary and secondary data and combinations of primary data-gathering methods as well. The way to choose between this rich field of possibilities is explored in more depth later in this chapter.

Each method is now considered individually.

Method: Participant Observation (often shortened in books and articles to PO)

Description / definition

PO is an ethnographic research method. This means it provides a detailed look at how a group or sub-section of society live their lives. PO involves joining in (participating) with the everyday lives of individuals as they go about their 'normal' activities, and observing their social detail as it unfolds (observation).

PO can be overt or covert. An overt PO study means that the researcher is not hiding her or his identity as a researcher from the group studies. The researcher is open about their role in sociologically observing the group interaction as s/he participates in it.

A covert PO study involves some degree of disguise or even deception by the researcher, in that the sociologist's researching role is kept secret from those observed. This may mean not revealing the truth to direct questions, and usually involves the researcher in a far more involved form of research, as a role within the observed group must be found or the group may not accept the 'new member'. In instances such as these, the sociologist can be greatly assisted by a 'key informant' or 'gatekeeper' who provides an introduction to the group, either knowing the researcher's identity and helping to keep it secret, or by remaining ignorant but being befriended by the researcher. (For an example of such covert access, and its dangers, see *A Glasgow Gang Observed* by James Patrick, Eyre

Methuen, 1973, or there is a brief description on p. 2 in Morrisson's *Methods in Sociology*, Longman Group Limited, 1986. Patrick observed the gang for some time by covertly joining in with their activities, but had to change his name after a rapid exit because his role was discovered by the gang. The examples of PO studies developed below are both overt and covert varieties.)

Type of enquiry appropriate for

PO is most appropriate for, and most frequently used by sociologists seeking as true as possible to life a picture of a particular group's social reality. It has the distinct advantage of taking the researcher right into the thick of what s/he has chosen to study. Any enquiry where the individual experiences of people are sought, or where their re-telling in another way (such as an interview) may not glean the truth, is amenable to PO. Any study where the validity (truth) of the data is paramount will benefit from PO, as will a study in which detail and richness of data are more important than the size of the sample (see below for one distinct disadvantage of PO – the difficulty of generalising from the method's usually small samples).

Advantages / disadvantages

Covert PO – advantages

1 The group, remaining unaware of being observed, behave as usual in the presence of the secret observer.
2 Types of social behaviour that the participants may wish to keep secret themselves (such as illegal behaviour), can be studied.
3 The researcher can become fully immersed in the group and accepted by it, leading to a genuinely subject-centred approach: the group and the individuals comprising it become the centre of the study.

Covert PO – disadvantages

1 Sociologists can experience moral difficulties in covert roles: to use the above example of James Patrick, he became worried at his involvement in the violent behaviour of the Glasgow gang he observed.
2 Covert role study involves ethical dilemmas, as some researchers feel it is dishonest to deceive social members by keeping their observational role a secret.
3 Crucially for data validity, in fully immersed covert roles, sociologists can lose sight of their objectivity and become so accustomed to what they are seeing that it seems normal to them. In this situation the problem of subjectiveness becomes paramount, wherein the researcher may offer his or her own version of events which is biased from over-involvement in them.

Overt PO – advantages

1 The problems of ethical deception are neutralised.

2 Objectivity is probably more likely.

3 Problems of access (such as a 'native costume', which refers to clothing and skills which may need acquiring for entry to the observed group) are minimalised.

Overt PO – disadvantages

1 People may behave in a more controlled or disciplined manner as they know they are being observed. To an unquantifiable extent, the covert observer is always likely to witness unaltered interaction.

2 The researcher may be unable to fully picture life from the viewpoint of the individuals studied as s/he has not 'become' one of them.

3 A group could be outrightly hostile to an 'outsider' and either not admit them to their number, or do so and keep back certain information and behaviour through distrust.

Points common to covert and overt PO

Advantages (over other methods)

1 PO allows access to the inner social world of social members to a level of intimacy and ethnographic experience which no other method can arguably match. In some of the finest classic studies in sociology and anthropology, from Malinowski and Mead's separate enquiries early this century to Whyte's urban gang study of the 1940s, PO has often provided insights obtainable by no other method.

2 PO offers a uniquely qualitative view of the social world. If a researcher is seeking a detailed, personal understanding of the morals, day-to-day pressures, pleasures and habits of particular groups, PO is an invaluable research method if access to the group is possible (and this is not, of course, always the case. In such instances a researcher may turn to the next most qualitative research method, that of in-depth interviewing).

Disadvantages

1 It is difficult to generalise from PO data with high degrees of confidence. A researcher can only physically observe one, relatively small (certainly no larger than twenty or so) group at a time, and to do that in sufficient depth will take considerable time. Effectively then, PO studies trade depth and insight for generalisability. The sociologist can say a great deal about the people she or he studies, but cannot confidently assume the findings are representative of the opinions or behaviour of any other groups, no matter how similar their social composition may be.

2 PO takes a lot of time. Insightful, revealing data is the product, in some cases, of several years' immersion within a chosen social network. For this reason, as much as for any other mentioned immediately below, PO has to be carefully considered as a student enquiry method.

Points to consider if using the method

As the comments within Chapter 1, Basic Facts About the Project (see p. 7) indicate, careful thought on three main issues is needed before a PO approach is decided on for a student enquiry:

- Will access to a viable group be possible?
- Will any personal danger, or potential/actual illegal activities be entered into?
- Will sufficient data be gathered within the time constraints, implicit in a student A level enquiry?

If doubt exists on any one of these points it may be advisable to use another method. Certainly no dangerous or illegal behaviour should even be contemplated. Despite the understandable appeal of PO to many student researchers, it is much more methodologically sound to decide on the issue or problematic/hypothesis to be researched and then select an appropriate method, than to choose PO and proceed from there.

Example study – Cocaine Kids

There are, of course, many PO studies in sociological literature, and it is from among this rich canon of work that one recent PO study is briefly described below. This is done as an inducement to read further either this study or ones in this research tradition.

An excellent recent PO study (already referred to with an extract on p. 19) is Terry Williams' *Cocaine Kids*, published by Bloomsbury, 1990. Williams is a researcher at the City University of New York City, in America, and between 1982 and 1986 he spent an average of six hours a week among teenage crack-cocaine sellers in dangerously run-down areas of New York City such as the Bronx, Harlem and Washington Heights. Williams' study immediately illustrates two key elements of the PO mix. First, Williams engaged in a part-time overt PO study because he could not change an ascribed characteristic; his age. He was in his thirties at the time of the research, considerably older than the teenagers at the centre of the observed drug-dealing. This brought into play many of the advantages and disadvantages associated with overt PO mentioned above. For example, having an open researching role he was able to avoid the moral and legal difficulties of being amongst drug communities by refusing all illegal substances.

Second, another ascribed characteristic of Williams was a considerable help to his research. Williams is a black American, and the overwhelming majority of dealers (and users) are from the great mix of non-white American groups – blacks, Mexicans and particularly Hispanics. The book itself contributes to sociology's understanding of why so many non-whites are consumed in the drug sub-culture, and informs the underclass debate in which it is argued that non-whites are structurally excluded from opportunities open to white Americans. Hence, illegitimate diversions and illegal money-making schemes are sought instead (see pp. 200–1 and pp. 144–5 in Mike O'Donnell's *New Introduction to Sociology*, 3rd Edition, Nelson, 1992, for a brief synopsis of the underclass discussion. See also Reading 16 in O'Donnell's *Reader In Sociology*, 3rd Edition, p. 68 for Dahrendorf's views).

The significant advantage of PO as a rich source of primary data gathering is illustrated by *Cocaine Kids*. Williams introduces the reader to each of the main 'characters' at the outset, and is careful at the close of the study to document their fates in the rough world they move within. The gang leader, Max, accumulated enough money from a total of $8 million of business over three or four years (a long time in cocaine selling) to set up a legitimate business and move with his girlfriend to Florida. Two of the gang workers under him left the business fearing for their long-term safety, and when Williams last had contact with them in 1988/9, were working in legitimate manual jobs. One gang member returned to finish college, and the last member, Chillie, was shot whilst completing a sale and died some months later in his native Dominican Republic. Throughout the study, the reader is taken into the detailed world of otherwise sociologically inaccessible terrain. Williams ends the book in a style typical of this:

Today, as I walk through this city of fallen dreams and unquenchable hope, to the neighbourhood where I first met Max and the Kids, I see a new generation of Cocaine Kids in faded jeans and unlaced sneakers [trainers], draped with gold chains, their arrow-pointed haircuts topping fresh faces and hard-edged frowns ...

On the corner of 162nd Street, three boys and two girls shout to me almost in unison, their outstretched hands revealing their wares, 'got that coke, got that crack, got red caps, got blues, got yellow ones – you choose. What you want, my friend? What you need?'

The innocence of the young is lost in Washington Heights these days as a new generation of street corner boys and girls enters the shadowy world of dealing and prostitution. A new generation of Cocaine Kids is embarking on a voyage, searching for dreams that most will never find.

Terry Williams, *Cocaine Kids*, 1990.

Cocaine Kids is rapidly being seen as one of the most informative PO studies for some years, although one of the method's downfalls is its occasional veering away from theoretical analysis, and Williams' book can perhaps be justly accused of this. There is a tendency to present a vivid picture but to omit a sociological interpretation of it – this is seen as variously a strength and a flaw of PO.

A footnote on non-Participant Observation

In general, non-Participant Observation is best suited to more formal settings where an explained observer can discreetly watch interaction without needing a covert role. For example, non-participant observation has been used to observe gender interaction in the classroom, as it is possible for an observer to watch a school or college class fairly unobtrusively.

Two example studies here are David Hargreaves' work observing secondary school classrooms to explore teacher labelling of deviant pupils, in *Social Relations in a Secondary School*, Routledge, 1967 but also extracted pp. 43–6 in *Sociology; A New Approach* by M. Haralambos, Causeway Press, 1986. It should be noted that although one of the advantages of non-Participant Observation is usually not needing to adopt a role or gain access to a group, the negative impacts include the observer in some way altering the observed behaviour. Hargreaves experienced this in that teachers were generally more pleasant to pupils when he observed, which he chanced to discover from off the cuff remarks pupils made to him.

Also interesting is Dale Spender's work in video recording teachers' lessons to discern the amount of time spent on male and female pupils respectively. Spender achieved this form of non-participant observation by having a camera present in the classroom rather than herself, which may stretch definition somewhat but also enabled her to record one of her own lessons for analysis as well.

Method: Interviews (unstructured / focused / structured)

Description / definition

The interview is a commonly deployed tool in sociological research, and takes three differing forms according to the requirements of the particular researcher(s). Unstructured interviews lead to quite informal, in-depth type interviews where the researcher can follow-up on points that are of interest with the interviewee. The researcher usually has a few broad areas of enquiry mapped out, and possibly a number of questions, although the phrasing and order in which they are asked of each interviewee may vary. The prime benefit of this type of interview is the very qualitative level of data obtained from such an intimate 'conversation'.

The focused interview moves a step nearer to having a closely ordered sequence of questions. The interview will focus on a number of central issues, more usually in a set sequence and phrased in the same way for each respondent. Its main difference from the unstructured approach is to slightly reduce the flexibility for exploring a particular issue or experience that arises during the interview. This is seen to reduce the variation between the data gained from one interview and another.

The fully structured interview is almost akin to a personally supervised questionnaire. The questions will follow an identical order with each respondent. They will also have been carefully devised and possibly tried out on a small sample before the full data collection, to check for any confusing or ambiguous questions. All of this is done in the structural spirit outlined in Chapter 2 so as to replicate as closely as possible the rigorous and empirical standards of physical science. Proponents of structured interviews defend the method's high reliability on the lines that, as each respondent has answered the same set of questions and been asked them in the same way, variations in answers are due to varying opinions rather than differing questions themselves. This is an argument that returns sociologists to the heart of the methodological / theoretical debates outlined in Chapter 2.

Advantages / disadvantages

Three main points can be considered when exploring the advantages and disadvantages of the various types of interview available for research:

- The validity (truth) and reliability of interview data.
- The non-correspondence problem.
- The phrasing of questions.

With the first of these points, it is a recurrent positivist criticism of the more qualitative interview situations, the focused and unstructured varieties, that the varying question order or phrasing causes bias in the respondents' answers. This exposes something called the repeatability issue: at least, it is claimed, a structured interview can be repeated with someone else, or at a later date, without the worry that by asking the questions differently, different answers are being obtained. Those favouring the less structured approaches counter such criticism by stressing the highly in-depth and experiential information gained, which the structured interview overlooks.

There is a further issue here. From a phenomenologically inclined viewpoint, the structured interview is flawed due to what Pawson terms the imposition problem (Pawson, R. *A Measure for Measures: A Manifesto for Empirical Sociology*, Routledge, 1989). This describes how the choosing of particular issues to be answered by the respondent, and how these questions are phrased, has already imposed the researcher's viewpoint on the problem. The researcher can thus only learn about what has been narrowly expressed in a set of questions. This point can be widened to criticise the entire research process of interviewing, whereby even the most de-structured techniques nevertheless require asking (or imposing) questions.

The non-correspondence problem refers to the fact that people do not always do what they say they do. There may be a divergence, or non-correspondence between the answers a respondent gives in an interview situation, and the actions they actually perform in their everyday lives.

There is a well-documented tendency for the gap between what people say and what they do to become larger as status (social class), or ascriptive characteristics (age, gender or race) become more prominent in the interview interaction. Two classic examples of this can be followed up on by brief references as follows:

- The difference between past behaviour and current assertions at interview are illustrated in David Matza's work on young delinquents; for an accessible summary, see pp. 601–3 and p. 738 in Haralambos' *Themes and Perspectives*, 3rd Edition, 1990.
- A related point can be gleaned from the curious study of La Piere, who travelled across America in the 1930s with a Chinese couple: see p. 539 in Bilton et al *Introductory Sociology*, 2nd Edition, 1989.

The framing of questions is a point considered in the examples of interview schedules below, but it is sufficient to outline here the difference in style of question:

- The open question can have a number of detailed answers which allow individual and varied commentary: for example, What is your image of God, if any?

- The closed or fixed choice question allows only one answer, for example, How many times have you been to church in the last three months?

Some sociologists use multiple and / or pre-coded varieties of the closed question, each of which has in common the restricted nature of the respondent's answer. A multiple choice or pre-coded version of the last question would be:

How many times have you been to church in the last three months?

a Not at all   _____
b Once only   _____
c Two or three times   _____
d Every week   _____
e More than once a week   _____

Tick one answer only.

The open question obviously gleans data of a more qualitative nature and is hence more common in fairly unstructured interviews, although researchers typically build up an interview schedule from a variety of open and closed questions. Traditionally positivist researchers are more inclined to favour closed type questions so as to minimalise potential problems of validity and repeatability discussed above.

Type of enquiry appropriate for

Naturally, the three types of interview will lend themselves to particular types of enquiry. This can be shown diagrammatically as below:

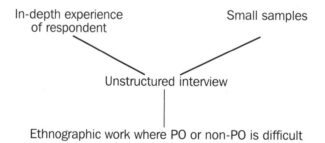

In-depth experience
of respondent

Small samples

Unstructured interview

Ethnographic work where PO or non-PO is difficult

Examples:

- What is it like to be homeless?
- What was an individual's experience of childbirth?
- Why have individuals broken certain laws?

In each of these cases, the experience of the individual is sought but the use of PO / non-PO may present real difficulties. The deployment of unstructured interviews will enable an ethnographic approach to be achieved, and the rich, inductive data it yields to be available to the researcher.

Focused and structured interviews can be used for much the same types of enquiry. The variation between them is largely one of emphasis in the degree of fixation of question framing and order in which they are asked. The appropriacy of these more positivist interview styles could be summarised as shown below:

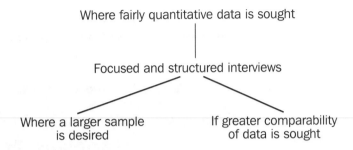

As the structured interview is often briefer it can be applied to larger samples. Equally, the unchanging form of the questions enables more comparison with other studies, or between groups of respondents in the same sample. With a larger sample it becomes possible to deduce, for example, that a high percentage of those under 24 years old answered 'Yes' to a particular question, while those over 55 answered 'No'. The conclusion of the researcher may be that, given that the question was identical, the variation in response may be due to age. For larger scale studies or those exploring more causative relationships, the focused or structured interview is more appropriate.

Example study

Below is an extract of an interview schedule. How accurately and appropriately phrased is it ? Would the data gained answer the researcher's queries without questions of reliability being raised? (Comments on these issues are in Chapter 6, p. 119).

An unstructured interview

The following is an example of a reasonably unstructured interview schedule taken from the methodological appendix of a classic sociological study, in which Stanley Cohen was in part trying to understand the effect of media coverage on public opinion towards young mods and rockers (youth groups).

Brighton Sample Interview Schedule, Whitsun 1965.

1   Preamble

I'm from the University of London, doing a study of what people think about this sort of thing. Do you mind giving me ten minutes to answer a few questions? There are no right or wrong answers – I just want your personal opinion. If you don't mind talking into a tape-recorder, it'll save time because I won't have to write everything down. I'm not going to ask you for your name, so don't worry about what you say.

2   Question guide

1   How do you feel about this sort of thing?
2   What do you think is the main cause of all this?

3 *Do you think that this sort of thing is something new?*

4 *Do you think that we're going to have this sort of thing with us for a long time ?*

5 *Do you agree with the way the police are handling this?*

6 *How would you like to see the ones who cause trouble handled?*
   (a) on the spot
   (b) by the police

7 *What would you do if your own child / brother / friend got involved in this?*

8 *What sort of youngsters do you think these are? Probe for:*
   – *local or out of town?*
   – *type of school?*
   – *social class?*
   – *'ordinary kids' or 'delinquent types'?*

Stanley Cohen, *Folk Devils and Moral Panics*, London, Paladin, 1973.

Points to consider if using the method

There are clearly considerable issues of potential bias to consider when employing interviews in project work. It is worth noting at this point that the sole A level researcher is not expected to attempt to gather data from over-ambitiously sized samples. Around thirty structured or focused interviews will suffice, with somewhat less for the unstructured or in-depth research method being necessary. As few as eight or ten interviews of an in-depth nature will often reveal significant quantities and quality of data to inform a particular problematic or hypothesis.

Method: Questionnaires

Description / definition

Questionnaires are essentially non-personal structured interviews. Instead of an interviewer administering the schedule of questions, the respondent is allowed or requested to answer the questions individually and without supervision.

On a large scale, for example where several thousand respondents are used, this is called a social survey. Questionnaires are sometimes distributed and asked to be returned by post, in which instance they are referred to as postal questionnaires.

In sum, a questionnaire consists of a schedule of written questions in a set, unaltered format which is filled in by an unattended respondent.

Type of enquiry appropriate for

The questionnaire is suited to work where larger samples are sought, as the method involves less time-investment than the interview and can hence deal with larger numbers of people. It is a method particularly suited to the obtaining of quantifiable data, partly because it is readily adapted to large samples but also because closed or pre-coded questions can be asked in considerable number.

For student enquiries the questionnaire may solve the problem of limited financial or time resources by enabling a sample of a reasonable size to be gained. Where twenty or thirty interviews would be a more than sufficient sample base for the project, greater confidence in the validity of findings could be obtained by using a sample of between fifty and one hundred with a questionnaire. If a considerable proportion of the questions are closed, multiple choice or pre-coded then the data evaluation stage (collating and interpreting results) is made easier by virtue of being able to count replies to certain questions. However, the student should be satisfied that this kind of quantitative data is suited to answering the chosen formulation of problematic or hypothesis. If more qualitative data is sought then the questionnaire, although it could be used with more open questions, may not be the most appropriate research technique.

Advantages / disadvantages

There is, in essence, a twofold problem with the questionnaire. Whilst in an interview a respondent may feel unable or be unwilling to answer certain questions truthfully, at least the interviewer can gauge the consistency and comfortableness of a respondent through having been present. With a questionnaire there can be no such interpretation of the individual's responses. In addition, any misunderstanding or ambiguity arising from the questions cannot be clarified by the researcher. These are both significant disadvantages.

On a broader methodological note, the questionnaire suffers from the imposition problem mentioned with interviews. The researcher has, perhaps to an even greater degree than pertains with the interview, imposed his or her definition of the most sociologically important aspects of what is being researched. When this is combined with the inability of the respondent to open up and develop personal lines of response, it becomes clear why many of a phenomenological disposition criticise the artificiality and validity of much questionnaire data.

Alternatively, questionnaires provide an arguably less intrusive approach to social research by reducing the scope for researcher bias in the interaction process. Whether in interviews or in PO / non-PO, the researcher to some degree has an interaction with the respondent which may alter the data. By collecting mainly quantitative data from larger samples, questionnaires are usually providing the basis for greater generalisation from the findings. They also provide greater confidence that replies have not been influenced by either researcher bias or subjectivity.

Example study

Many of the problems of the questionnaire can be illustrated with the complicated area of enquiring into human sexual behaviour. It is thought that this subject, more so than many others, can experience problems of respondent inhibition or exaggeration. The study below is printed as *The Kinsey Institute New Report on Sex*, by Reinisch, J.M. and Beasley, R., Penguin, 1990. Both authors work at the

Kinsey Institute for Research in Sex, Gender and Reproduction at Indiana University in the USA.

Before looking at this study, something needs briefly saying about the Kinsey Institute by way of introduction. In 1938 a Harvard trained scientist, Dr. Alfred C. Kinsey, was asked by Indiana University to provide a course in human sexuality. Kinsey rapidly found a dearth of material on the subject and so began generating his own through face-to-face interviews. By 1941 Kinsey received financial backing for his now growing research, and by 1947 he had established the Kinsey Institute to further the work. By 1953 Kinsey had conducted over 11,000 interviews, 5000 with males and 6000 with females, with the results published to sensational opinion in two volumes: *Sexual Behaviour in the Human Male*, 1948, and *Sexual Behaviour in the Human Female*, 1953. The results, the first detailed and highly explicit findings ever available to Americans on a national basis, shocked many.

In the late 1980s and now in the 1990s, sexual habits have again become highly relevant, particularly in the prediction of the spread of AIDS. Even in 1986, the American National Academy of Science was still using the data (from the 1940s and 1950s) of the Kinsey reports to predict the spread of AIDS in the 1990s. It was this parlous lack of information that prompted The Kinsey Institute to conduct a full-scale survey of 'the basic sexual knowledge of a statistically representative group of 1974 American adults'. The results alarmed the researchers by revealing considerable sexual ignorance: the authors write that 'Whether in campaigns for preventing AIDS, guidelines for avoiding unplanned pregnancy...or information about sex and ageing, the facts are not reaching the majority'.

There were eighteen questions (twelve were in a self-administered questionnaire, the other six by face-to-face interview) and Reinisch and Beasley gave a grade A to respondents getting between 16 and 18 answers correct; a grade B for getting 14 or 15 correct, and so on down to failing those scoring 9 or less correct answers.

55% failed. 0.5% got a grade A and only 4% a grade B. Such ignorance, the authors conclude, makes effective sexual knowledge a key dimension of combating AIDS and other sexually related ailments.

Examples of questions

Below are five of the eighteen questions asked in this research. Many of the others were considerably more explicit and detailed about personal sexual knowledge, but these serve as examples of the flavour of this study.

(The answers to the questions are in Chapter 6, p. 120.)

1   **Nowadays, what do you think is the age at which the average or typical American first has sexual intercourse ?**

a	**11 or younger**	b	**12**	c	**13**
d	**14**	e	**15**	f	**16**
g	**17**	h	**18**	i	**19**
j	**20**	k	**21 or older**	l	**Don't know**

2   *Out of every ten married American men, how many would you estimate have had an extra-marital affair – that is, have been sexually unfaithful to their wives?*

  a Less than one out of ten b 10% c 20% d 30% e 40% f 50% g 60% h 70% i 80% j 90% k More than nine out of ten l Don't know

3   *More than one out of four (25 percent) of American men have had a sexual experience with another male during either their teens or adult years.*

  True   *False*   *Don't know*

4   *Unless they are having sex, women do not need to have regular gynaecological (genital) examinations.*

  True   *False*   *Don't know*

5   *Menopause, or change of life as it is often called, does not cause most women to lose interest in having sex.*

  True   *False*   *Don't know*

Reinisch, J.M. and Beasley, R. *The Kinsey Institute New Report on Sex* , 1990.

The questions were carefully phrased by the Kinsey Institute researchers in conjunction with the Roper Organisation, a national body of expertise in sampling and questionnaires. Clearly, the response possibilities in what are all effectively multiple choice, closed answers, enables easy quantification of the data. The wide range of answers on questions 1 and 2 particularly avoid the suggesting of a 'correct' answer, and in general the questions all avoid complicated or off-putting ('rude') language. The authors acknowledge that they have investigated an area of social life where methodological sensitivity is especially important, but are nevertheless confident they have accurately caught the American level of sexual knowledge because the findings 'are based on a nationally representative sample. The high level of response on all of our questions gives us further confidence in the accuracy of our findings. In the end, only an average of 9 percent of people refused to answer any particular question, which is very low compared with other sex surveys.

Hence, the work of the Kinsey Institute shows how such a sensitive and personal area of social experience and knowledge can be quantitatively investigated, although sociologists of a less positivist persuasion would refute the meaning of arbitrary 'pass' or 'fail' tests of sexual knowledge. It is perhaps, for instance, arguable that what people know is less relevant than what they do in sexual behaviour: other studies reveal considerable awareness of AIDS dangers and so on, but also show that people have not altered their behaviour even so. This line of methodological questioning tends to undermine the validity of questionnaire data. (See also Reading 9 in O'Donnell's *New Introductory Reader In Sociology*, which specifically addresses the methodological issues of AIDS research.)

Points to consider if using the method

In some instances, it can be difficult to decide if an interview or a questionnaire is more appropriate, or indeed whether the use of both methods would be advantageous. To consider the respective merits of either method, the student may wish to refer to an example of an A level student's enquiry into racial attitudes at a Sixth Form College. This illustrates some of the differences in data-gathering hazards, and type of information obtained between the interview and the questionnaire. This can be found in *Sociology Review*, Vol. 2, No. 1, 1992.

Method: Documents of life and personal diaries

Description / definition

The noted symbolic interactionist Blumer has defined life documents as '...any research procedure which can tell us something about the subjective orientation of human actors' (Blumer, H. in *Critiques of Research in the Social Sciences: An Appraisal of Thomas and Znaniecki's The Polish Peasant in Europe and America*, Transaction Books, New Jersey, 1979). Ken Plummer, in his excellent work on life documents (Plummer.K. *Documents of Life: An Introduction to the Problems and Literature of a Humanistic Method*, George Allen and Unwin Ltd, 1983.) refines this definition and writes 'The world is full of personal documents. People keep diaries, send letters, take photos, write memos, tell biographies, scrawl graffiti, publish their memoires, write letters to the papers, leave suicide notes, inscribe memorials on tombstones, shoot films, paint pictures, make music and try to record their personal dreams...They are all in the broadest sense "documents of life".'

These various records of an individual life, whether collected purposely for the sociologist or not, constitute the raw material of this method. It attempts to capture the detailed daily life of an individual through their life span. This is without the sociologist necessarily being present, as would be the case with PO.

Type of enquiry appropriate for

Life documents and diaries are often referred to as 'humanistic' methods. This means they study the universally human elements of experience, rather than observe life from a utilitarian (or purely functional) scientific viewpoint.

The method seeks, therefore, to explore and record individual lives as they develop. This is done in the kind of detail sought by others of a phenomenological theoretical base, who might also support methods such as PO or the unstructured interview.

Where life documents differ from the unstructured interview is in the much greater span of time (sometimes many years) over which they record an individual life. Equally, life documents differ significantly from PO because of the day to day absence of the researcher with life documents.

Life documents and diaries hence lend themselves to studies where small, possibly unrepresentative samples are not seen as a problem, but where rich, inductive data is the aim. They can work very well for a student enquiry. Just one possible application would be to ask four or five elderly people to record their daily lives for a couple of months, either in a diary or regular journal. Together with other documents the respondents might make available (see Plummer's list above), this could form a fascinating insight into otherwise hidden and socially undervalued lives.

Advantages / disadvantages

As pointed out above, life documents are an intrinsically phenomenological method. Criticism of them therefore follows many of the avenues already explored in this chapter, for other similarly humanistic methods such as PO, non-PO and unstructured interviews. This criticism centres around the following key aspects:

- Representativeness: life documents contain small samples in considerable detail, raising questions of generalisability from the data gathered. Some using the method have argued (Blumer, H. 1979, Frazier, E.F. 1967, *Negro Youth at the Crossways; their personality development in the Middle State*, New York, Shocken Books, originally published in 1940) that generalisability is possible where the individual(s) in the life document sample are known to be 'fairly typical' of the wider population being studied. However, this still falls considerably short of the type of representativeness more positivist sociologists would desire, and does itself require a subjective judgement as to what is 'typical'.
- Reliabilty: this is the allied question of how thorough and accurate the internal matters of the methodology are. For example, is the writing or collection of journals or diaries regular and accurate? If significant time lapses occur between events and their recording they may be less reliably rendered.
- Validity: this, broadly, is a query as to the truth of the data. As with other humanistic methods, there may be reasons for disguising motives and actions (where crime is studied, for instance), or errors of judgement and personal bias may enter the record of events.
- Subjectivity: a critical test of which can never be available. Has the individual(s) studied and / or the sociologist brought personal opinion to bear significantly on the content and conclusions? If so, it may be necessary to prudently regard the researched personal biography as an interesting example of a phenomenon, rather than a representative and accurate sub-section.

These are the fundamental tests which must be applied in discussing the strengths and weaknesses of this highly individualistic and qualitative methodology.

Example studies (with follow-up page / book references)

As Plummer states in an interview with *New Society* (May 20th 1988: note that New Society has since merged to become *The New Statesman and Society*), the life document method began with the exhaustive 300 page study by Thomas and Znaniecki in 1918 of the life story of Wladek Wisniewski (Thomas, W.I. and

Znaniecki, F. *The Polish Peasant in Europe and America*, New York; Dover Publications (original editions published 1918 and 1920), 1958. Wisniewski was a Polish peasant who moved to Germany and later to Chicago as an immigrant.

Thomas and Znaniecski document Wisniewski's progress from his rural upbringing in Poland through to the plight of a poor US immigrant early this century, providing both a fascinating personal insight and a new sociological method.

Life documents fell out of sociological fashion from the 1940s as sociology became increasingly dominated by structural functionalism. Nevertheless, many studies were generated in the fertile 1920–1940 period, and life documents may be re-emerging more commonly in the methods mix in the 1990s as sociology becomes less 'perspective' dominated, and less theoretically deterministic.

Presented below are a few more life document studies that Plummer introduces in his work:

Person(s) studied: Mrs Abel, a woman dying with cancer.
Author(s): Strauss, A. and Glasner, B.
Title and publisher: *Anguish, A Case History of a Dying Trajectory,* Oxford, Martin Robertson, 1977.

Person(s) studied: Arthur Harding, a member of the East End of London's criminal underworld.
Author(s): Samuel, R.
Title and publisher: *East End Underworld, Chapters in the Life of Arthur Harding,* Routledge and Kegan Paul, 1981.

Person(s) studied: The Sanchez family, a poor Mexican family from an urban area (Lewis had, six years earlier, used the life document method to research poverty in a poor rural Mexican family.)
Author(s): Lewis, O.
Title and publisher: *A Death in the Sanchez Family*, London, Secker and Warburg, 1970.

Any of these three would be an accessible and interesting piece of background reading for the student, considering whether to, or actually using, the life document method.

Also excellent for the student exploring the method is the extract from Goldthorpe et al in O'Donnell's *Introductory Reader in Sociology*, Nelson, 1988, 2nd Edition p. 54. In this extract Goldthorpe et al describe their rationale for using life documents in their large scale, quantitative study of social mobility (social mobility is individual movement up or down the social class hierarchy).

Essentially, the authors felt that this statistical data on a sample of 10,000 men should be supplemented with more personal accounts from a small sub-sample of the overall sample. As the total sample was over 10,000, the authors actually approached around 700 of them for the personal document detailing the individual's attitude to and subjective experience of upward or downward mobility,or remaining in their class of origin. However, only just over half of the selected sub-sample replied, leading the team to doubt the validity of applying these qualitative accounts to the overall findings. Nevertheless, the extract in

O'Donnell's Reader provides the salient passages where the authors explain and justify the use of personal documents.

Points to consider if using the method

Life documents are an excellent but under-used research tool for the student undertaking project work. One of the student researcher's main limitations is the resource based area of time and money. Life documents enable the collection of informative, relevant and original data whilst remaining within practical project constraints.

In application of this method, the student should show awareness of the sample size, validity and other debates mentioned above. The problematic or hypothesis being investigated will also need to be theoretically adaptable to this very phenomenological method: researching voting behaviour in the last General Election would not make a suitable topic area to investigate with the life document method, for example.

There is an excellent practical toolkit on carrying out documentary research in Plummer's Documents of Life pp. 84–118 (Chapter 5). This is particularly appropriate for student use and details the stages and step-by-step implications of researching this way. Any student considering or embarking on life document based research would be advised to carefully read this section.

The personal diary method

Personal diaries have evolved from the middle-ages as documents primarily meant to remain private. They are usually intended as a regular, even daily, record of and reflection upon events. Although the diaries of Samuel Pepys from the 1660s are probably the most famous example of the diary, the golden age of the diary was most likely to have been in nineteenth century Victorian England. It was at this time that politicians such as Benjamin Disreili (Prime Minister 1868 and 1874–80) kept hourly diary entries so as to be able to account for as much time as possible when facing the after-death 'interview' at the gates of heaven.

The history of the diary as a sociological method is a thin and inglorious one. This reflects two major methodological concerns that it is difficult to redress with the diary method – selectivity and typicality. The selectivity issue highlights the fact that the diarist decides what is included, not the sociologist. This could lead to irrelevance and inaccuracy. Maas and Kuypers tried to circumvent this problem in their research into the experience of ageing (Mass, S. and Kuypers, J.A. *From Thirty to Seventy: a 40 Year Long Study of Adult Lifestyles and Personality*, Jossey-Bass, London, 1974). They divided the diary day record into three time periods and specified what sorts of things to include. However, this solution may equally contain the unusual methodological dichotomy for a qualitative method of imposing a framework on the respondent.

The second issue of typicality describes the degree of confidence the sociologist can have in the usualness of the day recorded. Most people's lives follow fairly regular patterns, and if the diary period (around seven to ten days is the preferred time span) happens to be untypical, the researcher's picture will be distorted. Again, it may help to ask diarists to comment on the level of typicality in the time period evidenced, although this again frameworks the respondent in perhaps an overly suggestive way.

Despite these problems, pockets of interesting sociological work have made use of the diary method. This is sometimes combined with interviews so that the available data base is wider than that obtainable from the interview setting alone. Here, the respondent might keep a diary for a week and then discuss it with the researcher. This can enable exploration of other matters not included by the respondent and is an opportunity to follow up on issues of selectivity, typicality or content generally.

For the student researcher the diary method, or the diary-interview method, could be an original and interesting approach. The paucity of methodological literature available is a problem, as is the lack of study examples that exist. Below are three that could serve as working examples for the interested student: criticism of this method derives from an anti-phenomenological root common to the doubts on accuracy and objectivity / generalisability applied to the unstructured interview, PO /non -PO and case studies.

Example diary studies

Oakley, A. *The Sociology of Housework*, Martin Robertson, Oxford, 1974. Oakley asked respondents to keep a housework diary, revealing for the emerging feminist debate the sheer hard work and long hours housework demands. This is a widely available and readable study.

Lewis, O. *Five Families*, Basic Books, New York, 1959. Lewis observed five poverty stricken families in Mexico for some time, finally deciding that to record one 'typical' day in minute detail would provide an excellent glimpse of the day to day grind of poverty. The work formed the basis for the once theoretically popular notion of a 'culture of poverty'.

Chambliss, B. *Box Man, A Professional Thief's Journal* (by Harry King as told to Bill Chambliss), Harper and Row, New York, 1972. An insight into the criminal underworld from a leading American criminologist of neo-Marxian background.

Addendum on Case Studies

A case study is an in-depth examination, often through direct primary data-gathering methods such as PO, of a particular institution or (in the guise of the life document) of an individual. As Professor Jennifer Platt explains in an accessible and wide-ranging review of the case study method, the method '...has been associated with qualitative methods, with older writers having life histories in mind while more recent writers think first of participant observation' (Platt, J. *Sociology Review*, Vol. 2, No 3, Philip Allan Publishers, 1993).

Hence, a case study can be a study of an institution in detail that uses PO. One such classic study is Erving Goffman's pioneering fieldwork at a mental hospital in California in the 1950s. In a covert role, acting as Assistant to the Athletic Director, Goffman observed mistreatment of patients and many of the processes which produce a definition of insanity (Goffman, E. *Asylums*, Harmondsworth, Penguin 1968). Many of Goffman's original theoretical contributions arose from this case study, such as the idea of the mortification of the self and the labelling of the individual in total institutions.

Stephen Ball's study is another that falls within the description of a case study. Ball used various methods in gauging life in a comprehensive school from the viewpoint of staff and pupils (Ball, S. *Beachside Comprehensive*, Cambridge University Press, Cambridge, 1981). Using covert PO, interviews and questionnaires, Ball provides an intimate year-long picture of one comprehensive school.

With this study it is possible to discern one of the key drawbacks of the case study approach. Ball (and Goffman) conducted fieldwork in just one institution of the type (ie a school or asylum) they were interested in. As Platt states, 'Consider your own school or college and examine how typical or untypical it is. Topics which you might want to consider include: single sex versus mixed sex schools, comprehensive versus selective schools, schools with different catchment·areas' (Platt, 1993). It is readily conceivable that one school is only 'typical' of itself and not even like others of its 'type'. This brings the work of Ball and others in this tradition into three areas of methodological controversy:

- Generalisability: can the findings be meaningfully applied to other settings?
- Replication: can the study be repeated and similar findings obtained, either at the original place of study or another institution?
- Subjectivity: do the opinions and interests of the researcher, usually working alone, bias the data gained?

In this respect, the methodological shortcomings (and strengths) of case studies are very similar to those of other qualitative methods – especially PO / non-PO, life documents, qualitative content analysis and unstructured or focused interviews. The student should consider case study methods as an amalgam of the phenomenological approaches detailed in this chapter, and that the methods listed in the previous sentence form a 'methods mix' of options for the intending case study researcher. It is a method that can be fruitfully applied in student research as it requires a basic minimum of one major institution to examine; for example, a place of Saturday work, a sports club or leisure environment frequented a lot. The student considering its use should thus look at this section in conjunction with the others in this chapter on broadly qualitative methodologies.

Method: Content Analysis (often shortened to CA)

Description / definition

CA is a technique for systematically analysing the content and meaning of media messages. It has been applied to newspapers, magazines, comics, television programmes and films by various sociologists.

CA leads the researcher to encode the content of the medium studied: to, in other words, break the content down into recorded sections or types. For example, considerable work has been done using CA to investigate the images of women in the media (see the example studies below), which has often involved counting the types of role women are portrayed in. How many stereotypical housewives are portrayed? How many women are in positions of authority and high status? As Ros Gill has commented (*Social Studies Review*, September 1988) of Tuchman's 1977 CA study, '...on primetime TV men outnumbered women by three to one. Only 6% of adverts have female voice-overs – women's voices, advertisers argued, "lack authority even in the domestic sphere".' In the same article, Ros Gill points out that by the late 1980s the ratios were hardly altered: '1987 figures, quoted in a BBC TV broadcast entitled "Putting Women in the Picture", show that on-screen, men now outnumber women by "only" two to one'.

By this method the researcher aims to acquire an objective measure of what most people absorb incredibly quickly, in order to understand its possible influence on social attitudes and perception. It is possible, for example, that a greater variety and accuracy of imagery of women, could lead to more flexible views of gender generally in an audience.

There is a broad distinction to be drawn between CA at two periods in its methodological development.

In the 1970s and early 1980s CA was a largely quantitative method. This derived from the American model of objective, empiricist sociology and attempted to 'code' the programme, newspaper or magazine. This means the researcher would decide which categories to look for (for example, number of images of women as subordinate to men in any given text), and then seek to count them so as to obtain statistical understanding of the imagery.

This gave way in the late 1980s and 1990s to a more qualitative textual analysis which concerns itself more with the meanings of the presentations. Instead of counting types of images, this more recent textual analysis aims to elicit the underlying messages of media content. Following the pioneering work of Stuart Hall on 'the ideological effect' of television (1980), researchers sought to analyse the potentially narrow or biased range of views presented in the mass media. This work still sees the CA researcher exploring media output, from magazines to news programmes, although far more in the style of an alien trying to make sense of the messages. Using many of the techniques of film criticism and language analysis used in communication studies, qualitative CA breaks down the cultural content of a given media message.

This has recently involved feminist researchers such as Angela McRobbie (198?) in decoding the content of early teen female magazines such as *Jackie*, to uncover the construction of female behaviour it encourages in its young readers. Other targets for analysis have been news programmes and the world-view they impart to their audience.

Type of enquiry appropriate for

CA is usually applied to studies where the products of the media are a central concern. It would be possible to do a CA of almost any cultural product: a novel, for example, or a stage play. Sociologists, however, primarily concern themselves with the most socially significant cultural products of a given era, and those are in the late twentieth century, unquestionably derived from the electronic and print media, radio, film, television, newspaper, magazine, comic, and even record or compact disc. These dominating cultural artefacts of modern post-industrial society are particularly amenable to CA as they are readily available, undoubtedly highly influential in many people's lives. Yet they are not frequently deconstructed for hidden, less immediate messages or meanings.

In the 1940s Robert Merton usefully distinguished between what he termed the manifest and the latent functions of social institutions, the former being the officially defined role. With the television media, for example, this *manifest* function is often defined (from the original BBC charter in the 1920s) as being to 'inform, educate and entertain' the watching public. By *latent* function, Merton meant the underlying or not immediately obvious functions of a social institution, which may with the media be to divert and disguise public attention from a 'true' version of events (a left / Marxist view of media function). CA can reveal these latent messages, showing that, as Berger and Kellner put it, 'the world is not what it appears to be'.

A pioneering version of this type of insight has been provided by the Glasgow University Media Group (GUMG) since their original study *Bad News* was published in 1976. This examined media presentation of industrial relations from a specifically marxian perspective. As O'Donnell has written: 'The Glasgow group demonstrates its findings on the existence of hidden "codes" or patterns of assumption tending to favour dominant groups in various ways...they point out in *Bad News* that in reporting industrial disputes, the media tend to rely on official management sources'. In subsequent work the Glasgow group have conducted a CA of the Falklands War of 1982 and the anti-missile protests at Greenham Common airbase in the mid-1980s, further demonstrating (according to the researchers) the ideological bias of television news output. For further details on the GUMG work, see O'Donnell's *A New Introduction to Sociology*, 3rd Edition pp. 420–1, and also article number 94 in his *Reader in Sociology*, 2nd Edition, pp. 727–37.

Hence, any research project concerned in part or whole with the mass media may be amenable to the use of CA as either the central research method or a subsidiary one.

Advantages / disadvantages

CA offers an advantage of particular relevance to the student researcher – it is a relatively cheap research method. Data is readily available and can be photocopied or video taped for detailed analysis. Samples of respondents are not necessary, saving costs of gathering and interviewing numbers of people.

On another practical level, CA is repeatable. This is an advantage that harks back to the structuralism / phenomenology issues discussed in Chapter 2. As in Tuchman's work quoted on p. 70, it is possible with CA to repeat the research exercise again at a later date. This enables the researcher to say, for instance, that there were x number of women present in a category of television show at one point in time, and y number present some time later. This comparative approach (comparing a given media product at two separate points of time) can usefully indicate a shift in imagery or presentation that may be overlooked in other research methods. It would be a perfectly legitimate A level enquiry, for example, to look at the way Angela McRobbie conducted her CA work on the teen magazine *Jackie* and repeat the study on either another teen female magazine, or on the same one, to see if any comparability of message exists.

A final advantage of CA is in its objectivity as a method (although this has been criticised as only an apparent objectivity). CA does not encounter risks of respondent bias, a hazard of the interview and questionnaire. Nor does it interfere with what it is researching – a newspaper or television programme is inanimate, unlike the subjects of a PO study for example. Especially in its more quantitative form CA has a certain scientific validity derived from this objectivity.

This is, however, a contested point. Critics of some styles of CA, such as Ros Gill, suggest that this scientific objectivity is actually nebulous. The researcher, often as an individual, selects the topics for research, how they will be coded and interprets the meanings of the content. This is potentially very subjective. For instance, simply consider the great variety of response individuals in a media audience can have to a particular piece of content. Consider this joke which was transmitted as part of a comedy night on Channel 4 in 1990:

'Question – what's black and white and unanswered? Answer – Terry Waite's poll tax form.'*

Some viewers were undoubtedly offended by this joke, while others will have laughed albeit with a twinge of conscience. Others still may have found it both inoffensive and unfunny, and some of the audience may even not have understood the joke through ignorance as to the person's identity.

How is it possible, given such wide responses to much media output, to be confident a researcher is correctly identifying the meaning of a media product? The more quantitative forms of CA may have some leaning towards objectivity, but in the qualitative analysis of ideological message, CA arguably shares many of the methodological hazards of other broadly phenomenological techniques, such as PO and the less structured interviews.

Another negative feature of CA is the method's assumption that the media does have an impact on its audience of some lasting significance. Not only is diversity of audience reaction a common research finding, there is the further point that long-term impressions on the audience, from media content, have not been causally established (see the earlier discussion p. 25–6 in Chapter 2 on media effects). A valid criticism of much Marxian CA, such as that of the GUMG, is that people form their opinions (political or otherwise) from many sources of information and not just the media. Friends, personal experience and so on arguably also play a significant role in what a person thinks of a strike or a government policy. This suggests a theoretical dependency to CA which arguably weakens the method: in other words, it relies on a theoretical assumption that may be questionable, that the media does influence its audience.

Finally, CA can be criticised for leaving out the audience. (There is now a swing towards audience research, however. See Reading 79 in O'Donnell's *Reader In Sociology*, 3rd Edition.) The CA research process does not normally consider the actual audiences themselves by, for example, group discussion with a sample. This further erodes the objectivity of the researcher's analyses as they must remain the conclusions of, arguably, purely him or her. One very effective student project corrected for this by firstly conducting a CA on female magazines aimed at 16 to 24 year olds (*More, 17, 19* etc), and then interviewing a sample of readers to see if they viewed the products in a different way. Combining CA with another method like this can overcome a disadvantage such as audience omission.

* Terry Waite, the Church of England special envoy, was held captive in the Lebanon from 1987 to late 1991.

Example studies

The two studies given here as CA examples are chosen as being accessible and also derive from two different forms of mass media. In 1983 Angela McRobbie conducted a mainly qualitative CA of the teenage female comic / magazine *Jackie*. McRobbie's intention was to explore the presentation of femininity (or femaleness) that 'Jackie' imparts to its young readership of usually, females aged 10 to 14. McRobbie dissects the magazine to ascertain its normal format (for example, the regular use of a pin-up male in the centre pages, almost always a tall, 'hunky' pop or film star) and to gauge its message to its readership. Most articles, McRobbie found, concentrated on a limited number of recurrent issues:

a How to look good – advice on make-up, clothes, and other aspects of appearance.

b How to attract a boyfriend or 'fella' – this is presented as a primary task of the adolescent female.

c How to keep the 'hunky fella' once he is snared – this involves competition from (possibly) female friends being kept at bay.

McRobbie's conclusion is that *Jackie* promotes an 'ideology of adolescent femininity', a packaging of what young girls should look like and do, which revolves around the basically restricting (compared to getting, for example, qualifications and a career) task of finding a boyfriend. Hence, the myriad articles on kissing technique, 'how far to go' and when, and so on are all defining the intellectual and social limits of females in their early teens. McRobbie suggests this construct of 'romantic individualism' may be a partial explanation for female underachievement in certain school subjects and, subsequently, in the employment market.

McRobbie's study combines residual elements of the older style of CA in that she systematically counts the number and type of image / text in the selection of magazines examined. In also deducing an 'adolescent ideology' from these samples, McRobbie successfully deconstructs what many would purport to be a harmless, fun magazine. It is a very strong example of CA at its best, and an excellent further reference for the interested would be the extract in O'Donnell's *Reader in Sociology*, 2nd Edition, p. 737.

As an example of CA applied to television, an accessible and insightful recent contribution is Ros Brunt's qualitative analysis of the breakfast television show run on ITV from 1983 to 1992 (when it lost its franchise in the bidding round), called 'Good Morning Britain' (pp. 60–73 in Goodwin. G. and Whannel. G. (eds) *Understanding Television*, Routledge, 1992).

Brunt explains her methodology as a combination of the two CA approaches which involved 'watching a run of individual programmes for comparative purposes and doing some preliminary categorization and quantification of content...before moving to the interpretation of a single programme'.

Brunt describes the typical format of the programme as a mixture of serious news interspersed with more 'chatty' items amid a generally informal and purposely relaxed studio style. Brunt argues that to successfully deconstruct the 'world view' of any programme, such as 'Good Morning Britain', it is necessary to stand back from its assumptions, to make it 'strange': 'Textual analysis requires some degree of critical distance or 'making strange' in order to 'deconstruct a programme, unpack its constituent elements and work out exactly what is going on'. Approaching the programme in this way, Brunt finds its treatment of two items in particular, on the arrest of a terrorist and on the possible splits in the marriage of Prince Charles and Princess Diana, shows how the tone and content reinforce a conventional notion of 'being British'. Brunt argues this style excludes any alternative presentations, such as what the terrorist's cause may be about, or why we should be constitutionally concerned about the heir to the throne anyway. As Brunt comments: '...a royal marriage has no real material bearing on anybody else's lives and can in no way be designated "hard news", it nevertheless features in the media as a type of story which has the important symbolic function of expressing something about "the state of the nation". In particular, it "plays a crucial part in the media's construction of national ideologies, of Britishness".'

Brunt presents interesting excerpts from the programme as part of her textual analysis, concluding that 'Good Morning Britain' is ultimately patronising its viewers and making sure their 'world view' remains conventional and unthreatening. Her use of CA illustrates the method's efficacy for dissecting familiar cultural products, to access the latent functioning so widely unapparent or overlooked.

Points to consider if using the method

Looking again at the advantages and disadvantages of CA discussed earlier in this section, it can be summarised that CA can be a very productive student research method with certain provisos:

1   It may be wise to combine it with use of another method to avoid subjectivity.
2   It is really most appropriate for projects where some aspect(s) of the media are under consideration.
3   It may be wise to try the method before deciding on using it: Ros Gill has a stimulating exercise of CA of a daily newspaper within her article 'Altered Images': Women in the Media, *Social Studies Review*, September 1988.

Methods: Experiments, social surveys and conversation analysis

These three methods are considered together briefly here because they are less appropriate to the lone student researcher. This is not intended to be prescriptive.

As each method is briefly outlined below it should be clear why each may be very challenging to use in a student project.

Experiments take the form of a scientific-type procedure in social research. This need not be laboratory based, but has been so in certain studies. The work of Eysenck and Nias on the correlation between exposure to television violence and actual acts of violence is an example here. This work did involve laboratory experiments where groups of children were exposed to various violent television images of children playing roughly with dolls. The viewing children were then allowed to play with similar dolls and did so violently. A control group of children shown gentle play with the toys reacted by themselves playing gently with them after the video.

This work is sometimes advocated as evidence of negative media effects on viewers, especially younger viewers. There are, however, a number of problems in accepting it as such, and these illustrate some of the complications of social experiments. To begin with, humans cannot be isolated from their past the moment they enter a laboratory. These children would almost certainly have watched many hours of television on a regular basis before the experiment, and this inculcation must have had some effect on the laboratory behaviour. This effect, unfortunately, is impossible to measure. Further, it would clearly be unethical to isolate a group of people from television viewing for some years, even if a way could be found to do so (in February 1993, 10 % of a national sample of respondents said they would not permanently give up television viewing if they were given one million pounds for doing so).

Such practical and ethical concerns must be added to the arguably dubious general validity of experiments. For the student researcher several problems arise if this method were chosen:

a   Finding willing participants may be difficult.

b   Keeping within the law (a requirement of exam boards and good sense) may become an issue. Some experiments are quite ethically and morally dubious – for instance, the lost letters experiments of Farrington and Kidd (1980, quoted in Giddens, A. *Sociology*, Polity Press, 1989 pp. 140–1). The experimenters left letters containing money as apparently 'lost' in various public places and observed the characteristics of the finder to ascertain if males kept the money more than females (they did). Although the researchers answered their hypothesis, the legality of 'encouraging' theft is less certain.

c   Many areas of social science research are not suited to laboratory or other experiments. The data gleaned from them has been gained in an artificial environment, making questionable its applicability to everyday social behaviour. As much sociology stresses the culturally defined and shaped aspects of human behaviour, it is arguably methodologically dubious to measure social behaviour outside of that everyday social context.

Social surveys are the large scale application of the questionnaire to a hypothesis or problematic. Sometimes an interview is used, although this is obviously very time-consuming and costly with large samples. It is the size of the sample needed that precludes this method from student investigations – most social surveys question several hundred respondents, and sometimes several thousand.

The student could, though, replicate or amend a social survey which they have studied or have an interest in with a smaller sample of around 40 to 100 respondents. Just as one example, the Islington Crime Survey (No.2. 1990) provides information on crime not available through official criminal statistics. 1600 demographically representative residents of Islington in London were asked if they knew people who had committed crimes from a list used in the interview. The results provide an interesting sideline on the official crime rates – for example, 13.5 % of those asked knew someone who had committed a burglary. A student could quite legitimately re-shape such a social survey to the smaller sampling possibilities of project work.

Conversation analysis has become more widely used in sociology in recent years, but is essentially derived from models of communication behaviour from psychology and interpersonal behaviour studies. The tendency is to look at very specific types of interaction, such as courtroom procedure or police interviews, so as to interpret the construction of meaning and reality that is built up during the interaction.

Access to such situations will be limited for the mainstream project student, making conversation analysis a potentially misleading tool for research. Gaining data on very ordinary conversation has been done as part of what Goffman termed 'dramaturgical sociology' (a sociology of interaction in everyday life, as if people had unwritten but broadly understood 'scripts' to use) but this is a fairly specialised and in some respects obscure branch of sociology. Again, this is not to rule out the method or be prescriptive, but to point to potential problems given the scope of the student task.

Method : Official statistics (sometimes also referred to as social statistics)

Description / definition

Statistics in general are simply information represented in numerical form. Social statistics provide information on a wide range of social matters, from divorce to death rates, which can assist the sociologist in building accurate pictures of social phenomena. A statement from one official publication is that the aim of statistics is '...to present a manageable selection of statistical material relating to social policies which provides a picture of some significant ways in which our society is changing' (*Social Trends*, Government Statistical Service, quoted in Slattery, M. *Official Statistics*, Tavistock Publications, 1986).

However, as the astute student is no doubt aware, possibly no other single source of data is such a well-spring of controversy. From Durkheim's statistical treatment of suicide in 1897 onwards, the social sciences have debated the validity and meaningfulness of statistical data. The purpose of this section on the use of official statistics is to point to their considerable helpfulness but to adopt a critical methodological stance at the same time.

Type of enquiry appropriate for

Official statistics are available on many issues, which means they can be of some secondary data application to most student projects should the student choose them as part of the methods mix.

A brief review of topics for the project which could make use of statistics as a secondary data source is below. This should aid in considering which statistical sources can be helpful for which choice of topic. This is a brief, non-exhaustive list based around the A level syllabi, as most Examination Board criteria state the project must be syllabus-related :

- re-examining an existing sociological study
- family / gender issues / child issues
- work and leisure patterns
- class structure / change
- women at work / sexism
- racial discrimination / racism
- crime patterns / causes / criminal statistics
- church attendance / denominational membership
- voting behaviour and political affiliation

- suicide
- socialisation
- education
- class structure / change
- age and generation
- social mobility
- media consumption
- health, welfare and poverty

The Government collect statistical data through various departments, notably the Office of Population Censuses and Surveys (OPCS) and the Central Statistical Office. The tables below (adapted from Hakim, C. *Secondary Analysis in Social Research*, Allen and Unwin, 1982) indicate broadly which surveys would be of use to a particular project topic.

Survey	Relevant project topics
British Social Attitudes Survey and also the European Economic Community (EEC) Consumer Attitude survey	These measure changing attitudes to a range of social issues and are relevant for : – family / gender issues and child issues – work and leisure – women at work / sexism – racism – voting behaviour /political affiliation

Table 4.1

Survey	Relevant project topics
English House Condition Survey	– health, welfare and poverty – class structure / change – family issues – voting behaviour / political affiliation

Table 4.2

Source	Relevant project topics
Family Expenditure Survey and also the General Household Survey	These two surveys collect detailed information on the spending, leisure and life-style arrangements of a large panel of UK households. The General Household Survey is the more flexible of the two, and is regularly altered slightly to collect data on contemporarily relevant social issues. The data from these surveys is appropriate for projects in the areas of : – family / gender issues / child issues – health, welfare and poverty – social mobility – work and leisure patterns – education (to assess, for instance, the possible correlation between social class background and home life on educational attainment)

Table 4.3

Source	Relevant project topics
National Food Survey and also the Survey of Personal Incomes	These two surveys provide data on the nutritional and disposable income profiles of a considerable sample of households (or what the inland revenue term 'tax units'). The data from these two surveys would be useful in the following areas : – family / gender issues (for example, male – female earnings differentials) – class structure / change – health, welfare and poverty

Table 4.4

Source	Relevant project topics
National Child Development Survey	– family / child issues – age and generation particularly on a longitudinal basis ; in other words, a study which follows a cohort or age group over considerable time) – health, welfare and poverty (for example, the effects of poverty on physical and mental thriving) – education

Table 4.5

Source	Relevant project topics
National Training Survey and also the Workplace Industrial Relations Survey	– education – work and leisure – class structure / change – women at work / sexism – social mobility

Table 4.6

Two excellent sources of statistical data which are more generally available should these above prove difficult to obtain are :

1 Annual Abstract of Statistics, from the Government Statistical Service.

This very comprehensive source, one part of which forms an exercise below, covers a wide range of sociologically relevant topics :

- population trends
- divorce rates
- death rates
- birth rates
- housing patterns
- government expenditure
- income support payments
- pension payments
- employment, by male and female and by occupational sector

- prisons population and costs
- crime offence rates
- education, including – number of schools, number of students, number of teachers/lecturers
- expenditure
- personal income and wealth data

2 Social Trends published annually, Central Statistical Office. Perhaps more readily readable than the Annual Abstract, this contains data on :

- leisure patterns
- health, including diet, accidents and so on
- housing
- family matters

- population
- employment
- income and wealth
- participation, a category which details involvement in charity work, religion, the voluntary sector and politics.

Advantages / disadvantages

Many of the disadvantages of using statistics derive from a phenomenological viewpoint. As outlined in some detail in Chapter 2 sociologists from this theoretical stance question the meaning and validity of statistics. Even if they could be taken as accurate, which is doubted, what do they tell the social scientist about the individual's social world? There is a total lack of empathy and qualitative experience in such data that renders its use to strict limitations.

Questions must also be asked as to how such data is generated. The idea that statistics are lying around awaiting collection is false – they are created, or generated. This is a social process. What questions are asked by the government about health in the population? Why? What is excluded could be as important as what is imposed by researching teams. One key advantage of statistics is said to be their enabling comparisons between different places or times, but methods of collection and the questions asked change. How can such surveys be any more comparable than PO studies?

Despite these critical queries, the range of quantitative data available in modern societies continues to grow and it would be limiting to many questions asked in sociology if they were not to be exploited, even if this is done with methodological or ideological reservations. Other issues of the advantages and disadvantages of quantitative data can be brought out through practical examples of statistics in use.

To consider the usefulness of statistics to certain sociological research projects, a practical example follows. It is drawn from a widely available source and could make valuable, up-to-date secondary data for project work.

Statistics in action

Example : the death rate this century in Scotland

Tables 5 and 6 published in 1992 and containing data to the latest available year, 1990 are from the Central Statistical Office, a department of the Government's HMSO (Her Majesty's Stationery Office). The first table shows average numbers of male deaths in Scotland for three years in each decade from 1900 to 1982 and then for each year from 1969 to 1990.

Deaths: analysis by age and sex
Scotland Annual averages or calendar years

Males	All ages *	Under 1 year	1–4	5–9	10–14	15–19	20–24	25–34	35–44	45–54	55–64	65–74	75–84	85 and over
1900–02	40 224	9 189	4 798	1 083	672	1 069	1 292	2 506	2 935	3 591	4 597	4 531	3 117	834
1910–12	35 981	7 510	3 935	962	595	826	910	1 969	2 469	3 325	4 356	5 113	3 182	813
1920–22	34 649	6 757	2 847	710	489	747	791	1 616	2 128	3 314	4 785	5 624	3 298	911
1930–32	32 476	4 426	1 771	610	365	568	706	1 352	1 848	2 979	5 095	6 906	4 839	1 010
1940–42	36 384	3 973	1 011	449	321	668	888	1 643	2 090	3 348	5 728	8 556	6 317	1 337
1950–52	32 236	1 949	349	175	105	200	265	693	1 267	3 151	5 574	8 544	8 094	1 871
1960–62	32 401	1 578	222	121	102	146	185	456	1 013	2 865	6 682	8 505	7 980	2 425
1970–72	32 446	944	168	119	93	178	233	396	875	2 617	6 641	10 176	7 383	2 624
1980–82	31 723	451	80	56	71	206	233	423	776	2 280	5 601	10 152	8 804	2 591
1969	32 531	1 099	174	121	109	184	216	401	936	2 564	6 946	9 851	7 381	2 649
1970	32 538	1 010	186	125	90	161	232	403	891	2 604	6 923	9 987	7 266	2 660
1971	31 585	988	155	100	114	197	242	371	832	2 588	6 427	9 945	7 134	2 492
1972	33 215	833	162	133	76	176	226	413	902	2 658	6 573	10 596	7 748	2 719
1973	32 954	841	171	117	76	175	225	381	839	2 789	6 435	10 693	7 603	2 609
1974	32 722	748	148	97	83	202	183	403	953	2 739	6 205	10 757	7 505	2 699
1975	32 168	669	113	112	104	195	216	411	838	2 634	5 994	10 727	7 617	2 538
1976	32 983	568	110	84	97	204	212	448	811	2 621	6 109	10 926	8 146	2 642
1977	31 280	585	103	81	75	181	236	432	817	2 494	5 835	10 173	7 802	2 466
1978	32 432	479	87	63	78	211	210	479	854	2 508	5 888	10 734	8 299	2 542
1979	32 884	490	79	79	712	219	215	442	805	2 599	5 851	10 804	8 543	2 687
1980	31 669	481	93	65	78	190	223	421	778	2 316	5 628	10 248	8 571	2 577
1981	31 700	435	71	50	66	208	250	439	816	2 330	5 506	10 193	8 788	2 548
1982	31 801	436	77	53	69	220	225	410	733	2 195	5 669	10 015	9 052	2 647
1983	31 196	380	67	53	65	185	178	406	764	2 131	5 769	9 414	9 204	2 580
1984	30 731	389	87	53	65	172	202	429	696	2 017	5 493	9 337	9 222	2 569
1985	31 147	342	57	49	58	174	208	390	759	1 959	5 486	9 339	9 569	2 757
1986	31 111	334	66	44	49	177	238	436	757	1 967	5 345	9 169	9 574	2 496
1987	30 384	331	54	46	47	163	212	415	779	1 870	5 131	9 058	9 383	2 895
1988	30 195	324	64	39	42	181	246	475	808	1 915	4 997	8 763	9 314	3 027
1989	31 025	331	62	24	45	150	246	445	719	1 721	4 889	9 028	9 922	3 443
1990	29 617	297	62	31	50	138	240	502	745	1 734	4 512	8 635	9 499	3 172

Table 5

Females	All ages *	Under 1 year	1–4	5–9	10–14	15–19	20–24	25–34	35–44	45–54	55–64	65–74	75–84	85 and over
1900–02	39 891	7 143	4 477	1 162	747	1 058	1 246	2 625	2 732	3 130	4 485	5 273	4 305	1 508
1910–12	36 132	5 854	3 674	981	618	836	910	2 149	2 473	2 909	3 960	5 636	4 588	1 552
1920–22	34 449	5 029	2 602	687	489	711	889	1 947	2 266	2 828	4 157	5 587	5 443	1 814
1930–32	32 377	3 319	1 602	527	339	568	666	1 508	1 812	2 731	4 380	6 630	6 178	2 117
1940–42	33 715	2 852	921	373	283	595	656	1 382	1 672	2 528	4 630	7 674	7 613	2 536
1950–52	31 525	1 432	284	115	84	185	293	714	1 127	2 188	4 204	8 157	9 310	3 431
1960–62	30 559	1 107	170	80	63	72	87	287	762	1 897	4 115	7 752	9 991	4 177
1970–72	30 978	694	118	69	46	73	74	231	608	1 769	4 036	7 823	10 112	5 324
1980–82	32 326	337	49	37	44	74	73	213	493	1 456	3 565	7 781	11 333	6 871
1969	31 190	803	156	56	58	66	85	212	647	1 817	4 168	8 014	1 003	5 105
1970	31 102	704	129	82	50	77	92	244	632	1 804	4 108	7 814	10 158	5 209
1971	30 029	734	107	64	60	64	62	214	590	1 720	4 000	7 603	9 686	5 125
1972	31 802	644	117	62	29	79	67	234	602	1 783	4 001	8 052	10 439	5 639
1973	31 591	571	105	77	46	91	80	224	604	1 796	3 890	7 930	10 355	5 822
1974	32 018	578	109	59	48	73	90	217	613	1 741	3 979	8 037	10 440	6 034
1975	30 957	499	104	56	33	84	77	228	580	1 625	3 792	7 750	10 250	5 879
1976	32 270	391	86	48	49	69	88	235	567	1 708	3 916	7 961	10 795	6 357
1977	31 014	419	73	45	41	97	100	214	557	1 578	3 671	7 761	10 628	5 830
1978	32 691	351	73	37	61	93	86	236	598	1 651	3 871	8 208	11 028	6 398
1979	32 863	388	69	37	58	59	81	247	551	1 635	3 776	8 045	11 309	6 608
1980	31 630	350	51	41	44	77	90	222	547	1 511	3 587	7 673	10 988	6 449
1981	32 128	345	46	35	43	68	69	213	453	1 414	3 556	7 935	11 144	6 807
1982	33 221	317	50	35	45	78	60	203	479	1 444	3 552	7 735	11 867	7 356
1983	32 258	266	51	33	33	67	76	201	504	1 317	3 568	7 558	11 340	7 244
1984	31 614	283	62	32	37	72	78	205	475	1 320	3 703	6 979	11 134	7 234
1985	32 820	282	55	37	34	63	76	207	481	1 179	3 563	7 449	11 604	7 790
1986	32 356	247	50	16	24	50	77	188	441	1 181	3 372	7 251	11 476	7 983
1987	31 630	232	44	21	34	60	70	195	429	1 160	3 301	7 032	11 262	7 790
1988	31 762	219	33	22	21	54	63	197	470	1 115	3 250	6 879	11 361	8 078
1989	33 992	223	56	23	27	54	104	224	470	1 156	3 279	7 052	12 100	9 224
1990	31 910	213	32	16	34	46	68	204	468	1 099	3 109	6 685	11 233	8 703

Table 6

* In some years the totals include a small number of persons whose age was not stated

Source General Register Office (Scotland)

Reading across, the age-category at death is shown, getting older as one progresses from left to right. The second table shows the data for Scottish females in the same format.

Answer the questions below to gain some experience of social deduction from statistics (comments can be found in Chapter 6, p. 120)

1   How many 25-34 year old males died in 1978?

2   What trend in deaths is indicated by the data on all ages of male deaths 1900-1990?

3   What trend in male deaths is indicated by the data on those aged :
    a   under 1 year
    b   85 and over

4   What social developments this century might account for the answers to questions 2 and 3 above?

5   Do males or females tend to live longer?

6   Is this, in general, a reliable statistical source?

Points to consider if using the method

Official or other statistics do not have to form the whole of a student project. They can be used as an informative secondary source to contrast with the collection of primary data by the student.

If they are the main data source, it is wise to voice some of the methodological cautions concerning statistical information and to ask what shortcomings the data may have. It is also prudent to find out early on in a project heavily involving statistics, that the information sources exist and are readily (and cheaply) accessible. The sources quoted in this section are designed to help in this task.

Finally, bear in mind that slavish reproduction of existing tables, graphs and so on is of little value. Re-evaluation should involve re-representation, and bring original thoughts to a problem or issue as a result of analysing statistical data.

Method: Historical documents

Description / definition

This method of secondary data collection gives the researcher access to social experiences which occurred before his or her own lifetime, but in which s/he is currently interested. Sociology is fundamentally concerned with the modern era: with, in other words, the industrial period dating largely from the mid-eighteenth century. This still leaves substantial periods to investigate as the past, for example, a study of the emergence of the suffragette movement early in this century, in which women fought for and finally obtained the right to vote in 1918. This would concern a researcher with archive material of a written and photographic nature, newspaper articles from the era, government documents and so on.

Type of enquiry appropriate for

Documentary research is well suited to those inquiries where access to social experience is restricted to the past and must therefore rely on archive material, or where interviews (for example, with survivors of the holocaust) could be considerably aided by secondary historical materials from the time, or shortly afterwards. Weber's famous and influential study of the emergence of capitalism in Western Europe alongside a developing protestant ethic is an example of a study where the researcher draws upon religious records for an understanding of life at the time (Weber, M. *The Protestant Ethic and the Spirit of Capitalism*, 1912). Weber was writing in the early 1900s but enquiring into a social movement that dated back to the sixteenth century. Weber was able to combine a rigorous examination of written articles of the protestant faith with an analysis of records of increasingly rational business behaviour, such as the emergence of forms of book-keeping in the eighteenth century. These documentary findings supported Weber's thesis that a spirit of capitalism (a desire to make money) gained momentum from the protestant religion's growing acceptance of money-making as an activity approved by God.

A student inquiry need not be this historically abstract to benefit from documentary evidence. One student study of how women's experience of domestic life has changed this century, drew on diaries of servants in Edwardian households to support information gained from interviews with elderly women who recalled their personal experiences.

Advantages / disadvantages

Rather like content analysis, documentary research can accommodate both the qualitative and the quantitative types of recording social life. The student example given immediately above is clearly qualitative. In some work the researcher may uncover the actions and movements of large numbers of people, as in the Mass Observation Day experiment of 1937 (Jennings, H. and Madge, C. (eds) *Mass Observation Day Survey May 12th 1937*, Faber and Faber, 1987). This involved a large sample of several hundred different members of society recording their everyday activites on one particular day, the twelfth day of each month. This flexibility of documentary research to provide both qualitative and quantitative data is a distinct advantage of the method. Applied sensitively to a student enquiry, it could inform a project with broadly quantitative data which is supplemented with one or two more detailed qualitative documented experiences.

As has already been emphasised, documents are also an essential source of information where the researcher's work takes him or her back to the past. Even if only to inform other primary data, the documentary evidence will provide a useful backdrop.

However, the method has one major weakness. This is the degree of interpretation required when discerning trends or facts from the documents. Is the researcher interpreting something correctly? Is the evidence accurate in the first place? The method relies on accurate documentary recording at the time (which may be difficult to judge) and also on accurate and sensitive 'reading' of the documents by the researcher. These problems are the subject of an exercise at the end of this section.

Example study

An excellent example of the use of historical documents is Elshtain's *Women and War* (1987). Elshtain's aim is to explore the imagery and construction of gender in relation to war. In the received historical understanding of wars, from the ancient battles of Asia or the Roman Empire to medieval conquests and modern mass warfare, the protagonists are overwhelmingly male. It is men who, according to the official history, decide upon war, organise war and fight the war. Elshtain's contention is that this leaves out the role women have always played in relation to war. She concedes that women have rarely fought in wars, although there is small but significant evidence of this from a whole variety of epochs. Rather, Elshtain contends that history overlooks the role of women in wartime, ignoring the feminine experience of conflict. Just as Marx argued history was a 'bourgeois' obsession because it concentrates on the battles and power plays of elites, not the day to day struggle of the majority for material existence, so Elshtain believes women have been ideologically excluded from the history of war.

Her method as shown in table 7, is to draw on a very wide range of documentary material relating women's and men's experiences of conflict.

Era	Source
Ancient Greece	Plato's Republic
The American Civil War (1861–5)	Using, among many others, The Private Mary Chestnut: The Unpublished Civil War Diaries.
The Vietnam War (1964–75)	Elshtain comments, 'the Vietnam literature is vast'. One of her most poignant sources is Wallace Terry, *Bloods: An Oral History of the Vietnam War by Black Veterans*, Ballantine Books, 1984).

Table 7

The American Civil War was fought between the North and South of the country. The diaries of the women's experience at the time which Elshtain quotes from, reveal the struggles and sufferings of women during wartime which are not part of the official (male) histories. Many women sewed uniforms, made bandages, nursed the wounded and offered food supplies to troops to keep them marching. Individual lives appear in pain from the documents: Mrs W. Kirby 'captured and imprisoned as a blockade runner', and a woman whose entire family of husband and sons joined up to fight: 'Oh yes, I shall miss my husband mightily, but I ain't never cried about it; I never shed a tear for the old man, nor for the boys either'. Fortitude and resoluteness were demanded of women as well as the men.

Emerging also from the documents are records of tragedies that can only be imagined today: a roll of mothers in North Carolina who lost sons to the war reveals two women who 'gave' eleven sons each to the fighting, four who 'gave' nine sons, and so on down to twenty-two women who lost three sons in the war. This catalogue of suffering and loss reveals a separate side to conventional accounts of warfare, focusing as they do on fighting action, tactics and male support systems ('mateyness' or 'buddiness'). In one account of the war the grim reality of many women's direct involvement is starkly apparent. Moore describes the women who '...followed their husbands and brothers to the field of battle and to rebel prisons: who went down into the very edge of the fight, to rescue the wounded, and cheer and comfort the dying...who penetrated the lines of the enemy on dangerous missions (and) pushed on our sanitary enterprises' (in Moore, F. *Women of the War; Their Heroism and Self-Sacrifice*, Scranton, 1867).

Hence Elshtain is able to successfully re-evaluate women's role in war and offer an alternative historical formulation of military femininity to challenge the narrow view held by previous academic history. Her work is an illustration of the strong contribution documentary research can make to social science.

Points to consider if using the method

Availability is a key consideration for the student researcher. Will sufficient and relevant information be accessed easily?

A library check early on in the project thinking process may be illuminating. If this check reveals scant potential sources, it may not be possible or wise to pursue the chosen topic through this particular method.

Whether to use documentary sources on their own in a project, as the sole research method, is also a key consideration. This will require substantial use of documents, preferably from a range of sources. A project based entirely on secondary sources is quite acceptable but will only be successful if rigorous use of a diversity of relevant material is applied to the hypothesis or problematic. This makes the first point on a library and document check especially important if documentation is to be the sole research tool.

A more productive approach may be to combine documentary research with a method of primary data gathering, as mentioned above in the example of a student project on women's experiences of service life (being a servant) early this century. This requires appropriate application of documentary sources alongside data generated by the student, which many students find a more balanced and fertile strategy than purely secondary data work.

There is also a question of how documents are to be evaluated. Are they accurate? Is the researcher interpreting them correctly? Some of the problems here are similar to those of content analysis discussed earlier. This methodological issue forms the basis of the exercise below.

Exercise on documentary research

With relation to Elshtain's work on women and war described above, consider:

a In what ways might the accounts of women's experiences be open to question? Can we rely on them as accurate sources of information?

b It is important to methodologically distinguish between historical documents (which are about an era or set of events but which may refer to individual lives) and a document of life, which details one individual's life in detail.

How are these two methods different? Comments on these two issues are in Chapter 6, p. 121

Method: The mass media

Description / definition

Using the mass media as a secondary data source means it is a supplementary source of information for a project. The project may not necessarily be on the media, but on homelessness, crime or any other social issue on which the media comments, offers information or documentary analysis. Hence, the media may provide data which adds to information gathered from other primary and/or secondary sources during the project.

Type of enquiry appropriate for

Regular social investigation and commentary in media sources in the 1990s has covered many issues of sociological relevance:

- child abuse
- rising crime
- links between unemployment and ill health
- divorce
- sexual assault/rape
- health care
- religious matters
- work and leisure patterns

Using television and newspaper sources for up to the minute data can provide sound framework knowledge and also follow-up references. One student working on her project on the elderly read a Guardian report on ageing. The newspaper report itself was based around a recently completed British Gas sponsored survey (1991) of experiences of ageing, conducted by Eric Midwinter (a noted sociological expert on the subject). This was available free of charge by post, and the student found this detailed report a considerable source of both up-to-date information and ideas for her project.

So even though a project may not be concerned with the media, the information these numerous and frequent modern sources provide can be effectively tapped. A project dealing directly with an aspect of the media will be systematically analysing output rather than applying it to another social issue (see content analysis earlier in this chapter).

Media sources

Some regularly and easily available sources of media are outlined below. Students may be familiar with others and, like all other quoted sources in this chapter, should view those below as a starting point and not a definitive list.

Print

- *New Statesman and Society*: this publication evolved from the merger between *New Statesman* and *New Society* in the late 1980s. It still offers thoughtful in-depth coverage of recent and historical social issues, and contains publicity of recent sociological publications.
- *The Guardian*: a good daily source, especially on social issues.
- *The Independent*: another recommended daily source, although more on political and environmental issues.
- The tabloids (for example, *The Sun, Daily Mirror* and so on) can provide evidence of the treatment of certain social issues, for instance:
  - coverage of royalty
  - political intrigue / scandal
  - sexist and racist content
    (On racist content, see the excellent review of *The Sun's* treatment of racial issues in Searle, C. *Your Daily Dose: Racism and The Sun*, Campaign for Press and Broadcasting Freedom, 1989. This lively and shocking short book illustrates the frequent racism of Britain's most popular tabloid paper.)
- *The Observer* (published on Sundays) also has a reputation for astute and investigative coverage of social issues.

Electronic

- Radio 4 occasionally has programmes of a sociologically relevant nature, for example a group discussion with a few convicted criminals on why they committed their crimes.
- Channel 4 and BBC 2 documentary programmes are well-researched sources of social data.
- It is advisable to regularly watch a news programme throughout the A level Sociology course in any case, but such programmes (Channel 4 News being arguably among the best quality) can provide regular material on social matters.
- Certain films and entertainment videos can be relevant to a narrow range of projects enquiring into the cultural aspects of the media, but for most students film and video will be less important.

As an illustration of the prevalence of social issues type programming on radio and television, Figures 3 and 4 show a fairly typical day's broadcasting from 1993.

Radio 4 programmes of possible interest for a range of topics:

2 pm *Airing the Future*: could be relevant to certain media topics, such as the funding and future of the BBC given its relationship (sometimes thought too cosy by sociologists of a neo-Marxian disposition) with the Government.

4 pm *Wide Awake in Ireland*: may inform projects of a psephological nature (concerned with voting behaviour) or the ideological and social dimensions of the 'troubles'.

8.30 pm *Living Dangerously*: Teenage lawbreakers give their view of the world and their place in it: very interesting for deviance-linked projects, especially those evaluating subcultural theory.

9.30 pm *Special Assignment*: depending on the topic, these detailed and well-researched one-off investigations could be very informative.

Television programmes of possible relevance to a range of topics:

BBC2 6 pm *Scrutiny*: depending on the contemporary legislation of the Houses of Parliament, this could contain up-to-date information on many relevant social issues from social security matters, to examination of the financial affairs of the Royal Family.

BBC2 7.15 pm *Sounds of the Seventies*: ITV London 9.55 pm *Trouble with the Sixties* and Channel 4 11 pm *Ready Steady Go!*: all programmes forming part of a mini-industry re-evaluating the 1960s and 1970s, and of particular interest to students researching into the age and generation area.

BBC2 7.50 pm *Fine Cut*: this was a programme about the communication achievements of the world's 130 million deaf people, and would be of importance to health and welfare issues, micro-sociological studies of interaction and researches into stereotyping or discrimination.

Channel 4 7 pm *A Week in Politics*: a programme raising methodological issues on polling important for all students, but even more so where the research focus is on voting behaviour or political theory such as assessing pluralism, for example.

Channel 4 11.35 pm *Adult Oprah*: *My Husband Won't Give Me Sex*: possibly of some interest in the gender relations area, although more likely to be thought provoking for a student examining media influence and audience involvement. This show from America is one of the most successful ever in its agony/discussion format, and an example such as this would prove a fascinating target for content analysis.

Hence, perfectly ordinary daily viewing and listening can provide several opportunities to obtain up-to-date and stimulating media contributions to the secondary data-gathering process. Keeping a regular eye on the schedules can be very helpful to the development of certain sociological project areas.

Points to consider if using the method

Three main considerations are advisable when using the media as information sources.

SANDY SMITHIES **Saturday Television**

BBC 1

7.0am Champion the Wonder Horse.**(R) 7.25** News. **7.30** Children's BBC: Henry's Cat:**(R) 7.35** Wiz Bang:**(S) 7.50** Littli' Bits:**(R) 8.10** Eggs 'n' Baker:**(S) 8.35** Tom and Jerry: Greatest Hits.**(R) 9.0** Going Live!**(S) 12.12** News.

12.15 Grandstand. Introduced by Steve Rider. **12.20** Football. **12.45** Racing from Ascot. **1.0** News. **1.05** Rugby Union – Scotland v Ireland highlights. **1.20** Racing. **1.35** Rugby Union – Scotland v Ireland. **1.55** Racing. **2.10** Rugby Union – England v France live from Twickenham. **4.40** Final Score. Times may vary.

5.15 News; regional news and sport; weather.

5.30 **Dad's Army**: No Spring for Frazer.**(T) (R)** Classic comedy with the Home Guard worthies.

6.0 **That's Showbusiness.(T)** Mike Smith hosts another round of the entertainment quiz.

6.30 **Noel's House Party.(S)** Fun and games at Crinkley Bottom, with glamorous expat Stephanie Beacham a-visiting.

7.25 **The Paul Daniels Magic Show.(T) (S)** With Daniels Jr, Swiss cycling duo Anja and Adrian, singer Jess Conrad and actress Kathy Staff.

8.15 **Casuality: Everybody Needs Somebody.(T) (S)** But does Holby need Dr Bower? William Gam-inara as the locum waiting to hear if he's got the consultant's post.

9.05 **News;(T)** weather.

9.25 **FILM: Parenthood.(T)** See Film Guide, page 1.

11.25 **Match of the Day.(S)** Highlights of two of today's Premier League games, and news of the rest, introduced by Desmond Lynam.

12.25 **FILM: Phantom of Hollywood.** For the catacombs of the Paris Opera read the back lot at MGM, its threatened redevelopment provoking a murderous response from the masked, disfigured thespian who's been lurking there undisturbed for yonks. Jack Cassidy leads this amusingly silly telemovie, made in 1974, with various old-timers on view including Broderick Crawford, Corinne Calvet. **1.35 Weather**, Close.

Wales: 5.25pm–6.0 Wales on Saturday.
Scotland: 1.35pm–3.30 Rugby Union: Scotland v Ireland. 4.40–5.15 Afternoon Sportscene. 11.25–12.25 Sportscene Match of the Day.
Northern Ireland: 1.35pm Rugby Union: Scotland v Ireland. 4.55–5.15 Nortern ireland Resutls.

BBC 2

8.0am Open University: Science Preparatory Maths: Graphs; **8.15** Something for Everyone; **8.40** The Flight of the Eagle. **9.05** FILM: The Southerner. See Film Guide, page 1. **10.35** James Johnston – Amongst the Greats. **11.15** The Strange Affair of . . . The Pied Piper.**(R) 11.45** Donovan the Diviner.(R)

12.15 **FILM:** Show Business. Entertainer Eddie Cantor had been in it for 35 years when he made this cheery backstage musical based on his early vaudeville career. Made in 1944, with Joan Davis.

1.45 **Animation Now:** Colours.

1.50 **Network East.(S)** Including an interview with South Afric-born Mooseajee Bhamjee, psychiactrist and member of Parliament in his adopted country of Ireland.

2.20 **Tanhaiyan**. Episode 11 of the 13-part Asian drama, in Urdu with English subtitles.

3.0 **FILM:** Lady L Sophia Loren plays turn-of-the-century laundress who marries nto the aristorcracy, in lightweight caper charting the lady's adventures. Written and directed (in 1965) by Peter Ustinov, with Paul Newman, David Niven.

4.45 **The Sky at Night.(S) (R)**

5.05 **Figure Skating:** European Championships. Latest action from Helsinki, with commentary by Alan Weeks.

6.0 **Scrutiny.(T)** The weekly report on the proceedings of the House of commons Select Committees.

6.30 **Cruffs 1993:** Best of Groups.(S) Live coverage of the judging in the Toy, Utilities and Working Dog groups at the NEC, Birmingham.

7.0 **News;** weather.

7.15 **Sounds of the Seventies:** The Clothes I Love to Wear.(S) See Watching Brief.

7.50 **Fine Cut:** In the Land of the Deaf. See Watching Brief.

9.25 **The Juliet Letters.** The story of the surprising musical collaboration, between the rock singer/songwriter Elvis Costello and the classical musicians of the Brodsky Quartet, which led to a joint album.

10.20 **Moving Pictures.** The movie magazine profiles controversial Hollywood producer Robert Evans, who career mosedived after successes like Rosemary's Baby and tonight's Marathon Man, but who is now tipped for a comeback. Plus an interview with Scots actor Peter Capaldi, screenwriter star of the new raod movie Soft Top Hard Shoulder, and a visit to Lone Pine, legendary cinema location in California.

11.10 **FILM:** Marathon Man. See Film Guide, page 1. **1.15** Close.

Scotland; 6.0pm–6.30 Scottish Lobby.
(T) Teletext Subtitles
(S) Stereo
(R) Repeat

Figure 3 The Guardian, 1993.

ITV London

5.30am News. **6.0** GMTV. **9.25** What's Up Doc?**(S)**
11.30 Movies, Movies, Movies. **12.0** The ITV Chart
Show.**(S) 1.0** News; weather; regional news.**(T)**

1.10	**Matlock.**
2.05	**Hard Time on Planet Earth:** Something to Bank On. More comic misadventures of the exiled alien.
3.0	**The-A-Team:** Water, Water Everywhere.(R)
3.55	**WCW Worldwide Wrestling.**
4.40	**News;** weather.
5.0	**London Tonight and Sport.(T)**
5.15	**Baywatch:** Rookie of the Year.**(T) (S)**
6.10	**Blind Date.(T) (S)**
7.10	**Barrymore**. Michael B returns with a new series of the folksy starring You the Public
7.55	**FILM: The Karate Kid III.(T) (S)** Yet more bouts of comic-strip combat, yet another reworking of the plot about an all-American kid (over-age Ralph Macchio) and his wise old Oriental mentor ('Pat' Morita). John G Avildsen directed this brain-numbing martial arts nonsense in 1989.
9.55	**Trouble with the Sixties.** See Watching Brief.
11.10	**News**; weather; regional news.**(T)**
11.30	**FILM: Angel Heart.** See Film Guide, page 1.
1.35	**The Big E.**
2.35	**Get Stuffed**. Followed by News.
2.40	**New Music**. Looking at voilent imagery in pop lyrics and videos.
3.45	**Rock Sport.** Followed by News.
4.0	**Coach:** Hayden's in the Kitchen with Dinah.
4.30	**BPM.(S)** Featuring soul singer Lorraine Cato. Followed by Night Shift.

Channel 4

6.0am The Wonderful Wizard of Oz.**(R) (S) 6.25** Spiff
and Hercules. **6.35** Alfred J Kwak. **7.0** Kideo.**(S) 7.30**
Jayce and the Wheeled Warriors.**(R) 8.0** Saved by the
Bell. **8.25** High Five. **9.0** News. **9.15** Racing: The
Morning Line. **10.0** Trans World Sport. **11.0** Gazzetta
Football Italia. **12.0** American Football: Play Action.**(R)**
12.30 Songs and Memories. With Sherry Rehman,
editor of Pakistan's most popular English-language
magazine.

1.0	**Victory Through Air Power.** This extraordinary wartime propaganda film, a personal project of Walt Disney's, combines animation witha live-action lecture in which military strategist Alexander de Seversky argues for long-range bombing of the enemy. It's preceded by Der Fuehrer's Face, an animated Donald Duck short which got Disney put on a miffed Hitler's hit-list.
2.30	**FILM:** Objective, Burma! See Film Guide, page 1.
5.05	Brookside.**(T) (S)**
6.30	Right to Reply.**(T) (S)** Behind-the-scenes on the BBC's magazine Good Morning . . . With Anne and Nick. Plus a studio discussion on Brookside's rap storyline.
7.0	**A Week in Politics.** How a new method of opinion polling may eliminate the sort of inaccuracies experienced at the last general election. Plus, this week's debate on rail privatisation. Including news summary; weather
8.0	**After Desert Storm.(T) (R)** Another showing, to mark the second anniversary of the start of Gulf War hostilities, for this Equinox documentary examing the lessons of the conflict, and assessing the role of technology inthe outcome.
9.0	**Stephen King's Gold Years.(T) (S)** Continuing the resistable sci-fi thriller, with Keith Szarabajka as the rejuvenated janitor, and a cameo appearance by the author, unwisely linkened in the blurb to Hitchcock.
10.0	**Saturday Zoo.(S)** Jonathan Ross's animal magic is unleashed, again, this time in an offbeat variety show combining comedy, chat, music and sketches. Joanna Lumley is guest cp-host, Roland Rivron a resident attraction, music comes from Sade and the all-female House Band.
11.0	**Ready Steady Go!** After the recent compilations, we're into a run of individual archive editions of the 60s rock show – this one showcasing the Beates, Hollies, and Martha and the Vandellas.
11.35	**Adult Oprah:** My Husband Won't Give Me Sex.**(S)** See Watching Brief.
12.30	**FILM:** The Twelve Chairs. See Film Guide. page 1.
2.10	**The Word.(S) (R)**
3.10	**Close.**

Figure 3 (Continued)

SUNDAY RADIO GUIDE

Radio 1

97.6-99.8 MHz, 1053, 1089 (285, 275m).
7.0am Gary Davies. **10.0** Dave Lee Travis. **1.0** Number Ones On One FM. **2.30.** Rockline. **4.0** UK Top 40. **7.0** Pete Tong. **8.0** Anne Nightingale **10.0** (FM only after 12.0) Gary Davies. **1.0** (FM) Lynn Parsons. **4.0** (FM Neale James)

Radio 2

88-90.2 MHz.
7.0am Don Maclean. **9.05** John Sachs. **10.30** Brian Hayes on Sunday. **12.0** Desmond Carrington. **2.0** Benny Green. **3.0** Alan Dell. **4.0** Sidney Torch. **4.30** Sing Something Simple. **5.0** Charlie Chester. **7.0** Richard Baker. **8.30** Sunday Half Hour. **9.0** Alan Keith. **10.0** Arts Programme. **12.05** Bick Barraclough's New Country. **12.35** Charles Nove. **3.0** Alex Lester.

Radio 3

90.2-92.4 MHz.
6.55 Weather, News headlines.
7.0 Sunday morning Concert. Featuring the BBP PO, BBC CO and BBC Singers performing works by Wagner, Ronald Finch, Moyzes, Lambert, Eugene Gossessens, Handel arr Harty, Arthur Benjamin, Lord Berners.
9.0 News: Brian Kay's Sunday Morning. Including **9.37** Artist of the Week: Regine Crespin (so-prano), performing Offenbach's Dis moi, Venus from La belle Helene; **11.21** Composer of the Week preview – Fuciks: Waltz, Ballerinas; plus, works by Moeran, Fux, Scott Joplin, Stravinsky, Praetorius, Debussy, Skempton, Luigini, Mozart, Rossini, Bach, Schubert, Gershwin.
12.0 Spirit of the Age. Profile of the violinist Catherine Mackintosh.
6.40 Out of the Mist. The extraordinary late flowering of Janacek's creative life.
7.30 Music for Chorus. BBC Singers/Simon Joly, with John Alley (piano), Susan Milan (flute), Sioned Williams (harp), Malcolm Hicks (organ). Elegy on the death of my daughter Olga; Kaspar Rucky; Potulny Silenec from The Wandering Madman; Otcenas from Moravian Our Father.
8.20 Prague Today. Translator Jin Josek surveys the revitalised cultural scene in Prague.
8.40 Music for Orchestra; Violin Concerto – Pilgrim-age of the soul; Sinfonietta. Ernst Kovacic (voilin), BBC SO/Andrew Davies.
9.45 Sunday Play: Dalliance, by Tom Stoppard, adapted from the play by Arthur Schnitzler. See listening Brief.
11.05 Music in Our Time. London Sinfonietta/Diego Masson. Simon Bainbridge; Concertante in moto perpetuo. Jonathan Lloyd; Waiting for Gozo. Mark Anthony Turnage. On all fours. Colin Matthrews: Contraflow. Xenakis: Thaallein.
12.0 Kindertotenlieder. Mahler's song-cycle in a vintage recording by Dame Jant Baker.
12.30 News; Close.

Radio 4

92.4-94.6 Mhz; 198 KHz (1514am).
5.55 Shipping. **6.0** News Briefing. **6.10** Prelude. **6.30** Morning Has Broken. **7.0** News. **7.10** Sunday Papers. **7.15** On Your Farm.
7.40 Sunday, with **8.0** News. **8.10** Sunday Papers.
8.50 Appeal. **9.0** News. **9.10** Sunday Papers.
9.15 Letter from America, by Alistar Cooke.
9.30 Morning Service. **10.15** The Archers. Omnibus
11.15 News Stand. **11.30** Pic of the Week.
12.15 Desert Island Discs. Travel with Dervla Murphy.
1.0 The World This Weekend.
2.0 Airing the Future. Michael Buerk chairs a debate on the future of the BBC. See Listening Brief.
4.0 Wide Awake in Ireland. John Walters looks at the elements that make Irish politics unique (R)
4.47 Welcome to My Wireless with veteran broadcaster
5.30 Poetry Please! Nobel Laureate poet Derek Walcott on the cultural forces that inspired his poetry.

6.0 Six O'Clock News.
6.15 Loss of Innonence. misha Glenny onm his love affair with Eastern and Central Europe.
6.30 Word of mouth. Language and the recession.(R)
7.0 God in the Palaces. The growth of religious fundamentalism in Israel.
7.30 Bookshelf. Author Michael Coren on his new biography of HG Wells. (R)
8.0 Fourth Column Classics, with Simon Hoggart.
8.30 Living Dangerously. Teenage lawbreakers give their view of the world and their place in it.
9.0 The Natural History Programme
9.30 Special Assignment.
10.0 News. **10.15** With Great Pleasure. Sandi Toksvig describes her lifelong passion for literature.
11.0 In Committee.
11.30 Seeds of Faith. Life in Lockerbie since the 1988 air disaster. **12.0** News: weather, shipping
12.44 (FM) Close; (LW) As BBC for Europe.

Radio 5

693, 909 KHz.
6.0am World Service. Newshour. **6.30** John Leslie's Weekend Edition. **9.30** TinTin **10.0** Johnnie Walker. **11.30** Fantasy Football Legue. **12.30** Simon Fanshawe's Sunday Brunch. **1.40** Open Forum. **2.0** Body Talk. **2.30** Where Were You . . . in 1986? **3.0** Sunday Sport Aston Villa v Middlesborough **6.0** A Century Remembered. **6.30** Education Matters. **7.15** How We Worked Then. **7.30** Italianissimo. **8.0** Language Live. **9.0** Open University. **9.30** Box 13. **10.10** Across the Line. **12.0** Close. **4.25** Cricket India v England. Second one-day international.

Classic FM

100-102 MHz.
5.0 am Andrew Leon. **6.0** Sarah Lucas. **9.0** Clasic Romance. **12.0** CD Request **2.0** Celebrelty Choice. **10.0** Contemporary Classics. **12.0** Andrew Leon. **2.0** Classic Romance.(R)

Radio Wales

882 kHz.
7.0am News. **7.02** Sounds Like Sunday. **7.30** All the Best Tunes. **8.0** News. **8.05** Grass Roots. **8.30** Celebration. **9.0** News: All Things Considered. **9.30** A String of Pearls. **10.30** Play it Again Frank. **11.30** Firt Hand. **12.0** Mews: Chris Stuart. **1.0** First Edition. **1.30** One the Threshold. **2.0** With Melody in Mind. **3.02** Best of Wales.(R) **4.0** News: Ask Me Another. **4.32** Landmark. **5.02** Golden Money. **6.02** Sounding Brass. **6.30** The Compact Review. **6.50** Catchphrase Colour Supplement. **7.30** Caniadeath Y Cysegr. **8.0** A Voice for All. **9.0** As R2.

Radio Cymru

92.5-96.8; 103.5-105 MHz.
6.0am Before Bach. **7.0** Newyddion: Coes of Mamgu. **7.30** Taro Nodyn. **8.30** Bwrw Golwg. **9.0** Newyddion; Papurau. **9.07** Lluniau'r Sul. **9.50** Beti A i Phobol. **10.30** Stiwdio 1. **11.0** Newyddion; Cywair. **11.45** Oedfa'r Bore. **12.15** Wythnos i w Chofio. **1.0** O'r Newydd. **1.30** Manylu. **2.0** Garddio. **2.30** Graf. **4.0** Newyydion: Dwy Fil O Freuddwydion. **4.30** Caniadeath y Cysegr. **5.0** Roial Mel **5.30** Nol Yn Y Newyddion. **6.0** Newyddion; Ivor Novello. **6.45** Gair Ne Ddau. **7.15** Gadw Sgor. **7.43** Ar Eich Gais. **8.30** Talwrn y Beirdd. **9.10** Sglein. **10.0** Newyddion; Epilog. **10.15** Hwyrach; Heno Bydd yr Adar yn Canu. **12.0** Gweler World Service.

BBC For Europe

BBC For Europe can be received in Western Europe on MHW 648 KHz (463) and on LW 198 Khz (1515m) from 12.34am-4.30am at the following times GMT.
5.30am Europe This Weekend. **5.55** European Sports.

Figure 4 The Guardian, 1993.

1   Do not accept media content uncritically. Studying the sociology of the mass media should make a student aware of potential causes of inaccuracy or misrepresentation (intended or otherwise) in the media representation of the world. Always question what the dominant assumptions of the journalist(s) seem to be. Be alert for any partisan or biased opinion. The very best investigative journalism of recent years has often had to fight a ban to reach the public, such as Duncan Campbell's BBC 2 programme about a secret spy satellite called Zircon, or the ITV programme 'Death on the Rock', which queried the fatal firearms action against an alleged terrorist operation on the island of Gibraltar in 1988.

   The power of the Home Secretary to issue a ban on a programme for 'security reasons' has often been questioned, being interpreted by those campaigning for greater press and broadcasting freedom as an unjustified means of censorship. As researching sociologists, it indicates a need for caution sometimes in reading and viewing what does come through to the public's attention.

2   Students are sometimes unsure if video or tape material can be presented in a context as part of the background discussion. Generally, the answer is no.

   If the student is studying an aspect of media output, such video or tape material may form part of the methodology but would still not be directly included in the context data. This is because video/tape material can be presented in addition to but not instead of written data. Hence, if a particularly relevant electronic media contribution merits inclusion for a project, the key parts will have to be transcribed: in other words, written down from a recording of the programme. This does not apply to the print media where a newspaper article can be included altogether or quoted from, giving the source and date as explained above.

   If a transcribed extract is used, make sure the date and channel of the programme are included after each transcribed extract. For a good example of this procedure, see the extract from the Glasgow University Media Group's Greenham study in O'Donnell's *Reader in Sociology*, Nelson, 2nd Edition, pp. 727–37.

3   It bears re-emphasising that, even if a project is directly investigating the media, the media itself is only one source among other secondary ones for background data. Good research practise involves the student in more than one secondary data source.

Combining methods (triangulation)

As this chapter on the various research methods has revealed, each has its specific limitations. For this reason a number of sociological studies make use of a combination of methods to compensate for one method's disadvantages by the use of another. This is often referred to as triangulation. Eileen Barker's popular study of the Unification Church (Barker, E. *The Professional Stranger*, Open University Press, 1981, see pp. 551–2 in Bilton et al *Introductory Sociology*, 2nd Edition, Macmillan 1989) is frequently cited as an example of the positive use of three different methods to rigorously research a challenging research question. Barker offers a strong justification for using PO, in-depth interviews and questionnaires for breadth and accuracy in her research.

Another motive for triangulation is to bridge the arguably artificial theoretical division in sociology between qualitative and quantitative data. The Hite Reports are an illustration of a successful bridging of this divide.

Hite has stated her desire to produce quantitative as well as qualitative presentations of data on human sexual and emotional experience. Her specific aim in the Hite Reports was to 'Devise a new methodological framework for analysis and presentation of data in mixed qualitative / quantitative research' (outlined in a paper presented to the American Association ior the Advancement of Science, Washington 1985).

As Hite stated: '...although quantification was necessary as part of the final result, a simple multiple choice questionnaire could not be used'. Hite's (revolutionary) intention was to ask women how they *feel* about sex and love, not how male researchers *think* women feel about sex and love. This meant allowing space for the respondent to develop an answer to each question. This is why large sections of the findings are respondents' personal verbatim replies in the Hite Reports.

The examples below are the best way to illustrate this 'essay-style answer' method. Figure 5 is part of the third section of the questionnaire for the third Hite Report (1991). This set of questions enquire about the respondent's current relationship. As a reading of Figure 5 will indicate, they are open-ended questions which can be answered in considerable detail and length, often including anecdotal evidence from the relationship.

Questionnaire

Your current relationship

26 **Are you in a relationship now? For how long? Do you live together? Are you married? Do you have children?**

27 **What is the most important part of this relationship, the reason you want it? Is it love, passion, sexual intimacy, economics, daily companionship, or the long-term value of a family relationship? Other?**

28 **Are you happy with the relationship? Inspired? What do you like most and least about it? Can you imagine spending the rest of your life in it? Is your partner happy?**

29 **Are you 'in love'? Or do you love them, more than being 'in love'? What kind of love do you feel?**

30 **Do you love your partner as much as s/he loves you? More? Does one of you need the other more? Do you feel loved?**

31 **What is the biggest problem in your relationship? How would you like to change things, if you could?**

32 *What do you enjoy doing together the most? Talking? Having sex? Being affectionate? Daily life? Sharing children? Hobbies? Going out? Other?*

33 *How does your partner act towards you in intimate moments? Does your partner tell you s/he loves you? That you are wonderful and beautiful? Very sexually desirable? Talk tenderly to you? Use baby talk? Sex talk? How do you feel?*

34 *What things does your partner most often criticise about you? What do you most often criticise about him/her?*

35 *What is the worst thing your partner has ever done to you? The worst thing you have ever done to him/her?*

36 *Is it easy to talk? Who talks more? Would you like more intimate talk – about feelings, reactions and problems? Future plans and dreams?*

37 *Does the relationship fill your deepest needs for closeness with another person? Or are there some parts of yourself that you can't share? That aren't accepted or understood? Or do you prefer not to share every part of yourself?*

Figure 5 The Hite Report, Hite, S. 1991.

Looking at just one question, Number 29, will illustrate Hite's presentation methods. This is a question about emotional fulfilment through and with the current partner. Extract 1 is an example of the qualitative treatment this one question received with just one respondent. In itself this shows the time taken to analyse the returned questionnaires; women not in a current relationship would have left this section blank, but several thousand will have ventured a response.

Extract 1

I fell most deeply in love with the man I later married. It felt wonderful and terrible. I loved him with the very core of my being. He was everything to me, my best friend, my lover, my intellectual soulmate. He was highly intelligent, full of fire and enthusiasm, a radical in his ideas, a lot of fun. The relationship lasted for ten years, seven of those in marriage. It was a union of extremes, we alternately passionately loved one another and hated one another. We were neurotics together, we discovered from the other what was missing in ourselves. It was vital to both, and through it, we grew, reached out - but perhaps too much of our energy was focused either toward or against each other.

Eventually the powerful chemistry between us, which was once sparkling and positive, became ugly and negative. And we parted. As we share two children and he loves them as much as I do, the relationship has never really ended: it is now a different entity. We have different mates, but a part of me will always love him. I see him every day in the faces of my children and he is still the most intellectually stimulating person I have ever known.

The Hite Report, Hite, S., 1991, p. 491.

There is a strength of feeling here which cannot be conveyed in the statistical tables, yet those tables reveal the broader pattern of women and their experience of love. The burning, day by day reality of one woman's experience of love (defined and expressed by her) reaches out to the reader from this extract. The reader can, at the same time, discern much broader trends on these sensitive matters from Hite's alternative presentation of the data from Question 29, as shown in Figure 6.

Here it is seen that only 13 % of women married for two years or more describe themselves as 'in love' with their husband. It can also be discerned that this is a fairly constant proportion of all women when broken down into soci-economic characteristics such as education, occupation and income. It also holds steady for demographic characteristics such as age and ethnicity, which could justify the conclusion that this 'loss of love' is a near-universal aspect of the American female marriage experience.

Although Hite does not use triangulation in the strict sense of combining two or more methods for one sociological study, she has used an interpretative and presentational framework which allows the individual to emerge within the wider picture. This is where a flexible approach to the practice of research can yield considerable benefits.

Statistical Data

Chapter 14

Is love passion or caring?

13% of women married more than two years say they are 'in love' with their husbands.

	Age		Education
%	under 18	13%	up to high school graduate
13%	18–34	12%	some college
12%	35–50	13%	college graduate
13%	51–71		
12%	71 and over		

			Occupation/Employment
		14%	homemaker and/or mother (full-time)
	Income: annual	13%	full-time employment
12%	under $5,000	12%	part-time employment
14%	$6,000–$14,000	13%	unemployed/student
13%	$15,000–$39,000		
12%	$40,000–$74,000		
13%	over $75,000		

	Race/Ethnicity
14%	White
12%	Black
13%	Hispanic
13%	Middle Eastern
13%	Asian-American
13%	other

Figure 6 The Hite Report, Hite, S. 1991.

Sampling Procedures

Sampling is an aspect of methodology too often given only brief attention by research students. Yet the representativeness of the people the sociologist gathers data from, can make a crucial impact on the accuracy and validity of the study. Whichever primary method may be adopted, the gathering of a reasonably sized and fairly diverse sample of respondents should be a carefully considered element in the methodology.

Much excellent information on the methods of sampling exists already in contemporary sociological material aimed at the advanced level researcher. The factual element in this section is therefore restricted, so that practical applications come to the fore. The student researcher should begin a familiarisation with sampling by understanding a few key terms and concepts:

- The survey or target population: this is the group the researcher aims to find out about; for example, women who have committed crimes (this would itself be a sub-group of all women).
- The sampling frame: the list of people from whom the sample is selected; for example, a telephone directory.
- The actual sample: this is the group of individuals actually used as respondents in the research, who should be as representative of the target population as possible.

There are three main ways of selecting a sample to ensure it is fairly representative:

1 Random sampling: this introduces chance in order to remove possible biases. Random sampling is a more sophisticated equivalent of drawing names from a hat – it gives a degree of confidence that the sample studied has been gained without researcher bias.

2 Stratified sampling: this goes a stage further than random sampling, by specifying certain features of the sampled individuals. For example, a sample of people to ask about their experiences of taking GCSE examinations will have to be:
    - young (the exam was introduced in 1988)
    - both male and female
    - from a range of schools or colleges.

    Stratifying this sample means the researcher could be more confident of representative views when gathering information on what taking GCSE's is like.

3 Snowball (or opportunity) sampling: this is when respondents are gathered as the research proceeds, and is usually used in PO studies where a sampling frame does not exist. For instance, Hunter Thompson's sample of Hell's Angels was gathered in this way, by hanging around with them, as they would not have been all written down as Hell's Angels on a list somewhere such as the telephone directory (the local police may have had such a list but would probably not have made it available). A good example of snowball sampling

can be found in O'Donnell's *Reader in Sociology*, 2nd Edition, pp. 49 – 53 in an extract from Ken Pryce's book *Endless Pressure*.

This is a very truncated explanation of sampling procedure so the student can learn from the examples developed further on in this section. Two recommended references for follow-up reading are:

- in Morrison, M. *Methods in Sociology*, Longman, 1986.
- pp. 26–8 in O'Donnell's *New Introduction to Sociology*, Nelson 3rd Edition, 1992.

Designing the Methodology

From the initial stages of generating ideas explored in Chapter 2, it has been emphasised that unity of hypothesis, methodology and evaluation is an essential ingredient of successful research. Having devised a hypothesis or more general problematic, the chosen method or methods mix must be applied sensitively and appropriately. Due to the complex set of possible method combinations, and the unlimited possible subjects for study, it is not practical here to detail optimal method(s) selection on an individual basis. However, the rigorous student should satisfy her or himself that each of the aspects of the checklist below have been satisfactorily resolved or at least considered and explicitly discussed.

Methodology Checklist

- The researcher should think flexibly as to the optimal method(s) to use and spend some time becoming familiar with the methodological facts and debates discussed in this chapter.

- The method should suit the hypothesis or problematic under investigation: this will involve consultation with the project supervisor.

- A preliminary draft of whichever type of schedule is to be applied should be drawn up. This may be a list of areas to explore in an unstructured interview, or a procedure for recording observation in a non-participant environment, and so on.

- This pilot methodology may benefit from small-scale pre-research application; this need only involve trying it out in one or two situations or with one or two respondents. This will enable student evaluation of individual questions before the overall research process. It could also reveal that the method chosen is not appropriate to the task being investigated without wasting large amounts of time and other resources.

- The researcher should have a reliable and appropriately non-intrusive method of recording results in place before gathering the main data: this may also benefit from testing at the pilot stage.

- Reasonably but realistically sized samples should be accurately selected for data-gathering. Advice as to appropriately sized samples has been included with discussion of the methods in this chapter.

- Data should be collected honestly, accurately and ethically. It should also be collected allowing good time for analysis and written presentation/evaluation. This latter process takes most students operating on an average post-16 study course around one month. Hence, allow (subject to individual project needs) about one month minimum for data collection and one month minimum for analysis and written presentation.

- When analysing the data, refer back to the hypothesis or problematic at issue. Does the data confirm, refute or leave unanswered or unclear the point being investigated?

- Be honestly self-critical in discussing the research process on paper. What went well? What was not so useful or may have biased or corrupted the data? What could be deduced from this about the research process in sociology?

- There must be an explicit justification for the chosen methodology that shows its selection to have been carefully related to the overall aim(s) of the study.

Making sure that these ten safeguards are met will reduce the possibility of sub-standard research. Flexibly using this chapter (including the follow-up references within it) to consider and select a method or methods for researching with, should result in optimal application from the sociological 'toolkit'.

*P*RESENTATION

This final chapter contains advice and examples on presentation of research data. Although not a major aspect of an inquiry, this is important for precise and easy understanding of what has been discovered. A common misperception is that exciting, multicolour diagrams can either compensate for poor data or somehow add to a generally sterile methodological procedure. This is not the case.

The purpose of the Results section is to simply and effectively communicate key findings to the reader. What counts, therefore, is the clarity of presentation rather than its appearance in itself. Evidently, scruffiness or error are to be avoided while retaining communicative competence as the goal.

Data of varying kinds are collected by sociologists. These include primary and secondary forms, qualitative and quantitative, and so on. The form of presentation must, hence, be suited to the type of data generated. Some common forms of presentation are:

- grouping of data under sub-headings
- prose extracts from respondents' statements
- drawings (for example, of a classroom's layout)
- researcher-led summaries of findings
- pie-charts
- graphs
- bar charts
- tables of figures

Two approaches that are not sufficient are:

1 Including, for instance, 30 filled-in questionnaires and labelling the section 'Results'.
2 Only including a video of an observation or a tape recording of an interview: an observational study and a transcript must be included. Videos, tapes and photographs cannot substitute for but only add to a written presentation of findings. With such recordings, visual or aural, care must be taken to consider any desires for anonymity by respondents.

Increasingly, students produce projects that are word processed with Results sections that are generated by computer graphics. This is not currently a requirement of any examination board, and so remains a personal choice. Further, although computer graphics can be very impressive, they do not always assist the reader in understanding the data if the student over-complicates the presentation.

Two of the examples below are extracts from projects which have been used for illustrative purposes in other chapters. The third example is from Student D in order to complete this range of Results. These extracted Results sections are used here to illustrate good and weaker presentation methods, and to give a glimpse of how qualitative and quantitative data require different treatments.

Results : Example 1

The first example of Methodology and Results is from Student A and is illustrative of both impressive and unhelpful presentation. Student A investigated a popular issue, that of unequal gender treatment in the classroom. Although frequently researched, this issue was thoroughly and maturely explored by this student. In places, however, the presentation could be improved.

The student introduces her objective for the study in her Rationale as follows:

I am aiming to see if teachers interact more with male than female pupils/students and whether this influences differential educational attainment. In order to find if this hypothesis is true I observed two secondary school classes with one male and one female teacher and two college lessons also with one male and one female teacher. In each lesson I distributed questionnaires to both pupils and teachers.

A glance at the student's two questionnaires (one for teachers in Figure 7, the other for students in Figure 8) shows that she applied her chosen method thoughtfully and with commendable attention to clarity of presentation. Although there is no requirement to present typed or professionally printed materials in the coursework, it is often the case that respondents take the student researcher more seriously if the presentation is careful and well finished. As this student was researching partly among her own age group, this would probably help obtain careful and thoughtful answers given the lack of a status gap between researcher and respondent (lack of such a status gap could, of course, be considered an advantage in itself).

Questionnaire for teachers

Please give reference to pupils' Christian names when answering questions.

Name: _____

Sex: M/F

What school do you teach at? _____

What subject(s) do you teach? _____

Which pupils take active participation in this lesson?
_____
_____

Which pupils ask you to explain further if they do not understand?
_____

Which pupils voice their opinions if they disagree with something you have said?
_____

Which pupils do you consider to work hard in, and outside, lessons?
_____

Which pupils do you think are doing exceptionally well in this lesson?
_____

How would you compare male and female pupils in terms of academic achievement?
_____

Are there any pupils who you feel you pay more attention to? If so why do you think that is?
_____
_____

Which pupils do you think may further their education once they have left school? _____
_____
_____

Which pupils do you think may get a job once they have left school?
_____
_____

What job can you see your pupils doing in the future, either after school or college?
_____
_____

Who were the first pupils you recognised in this lesson and why?
_____
_____

Can you see any children in your class having an early marriage and if so which pupils?
_____
_____

Are there any differences between the boys' and girls' behaviour in this class, if so what are they?
_____

Figure 7

Questionnaire for students

Name _____

Sex: M/F

Subjects studying: _____
_____
_____

Do you feel you take active participation within this classroom? Why?
_____
_____

Which students do take active participation within this classroom?
_____
_____

Do you, or would you if necessary, ask the teacher to explain something further if you did not understand? Why?
_____
_____

Which students do ask the teacher to explain further if they do not understand?
_____
_____

If you disagreed with something your teacher told you would you voice your opinion? Why?
_____
_____

Which students do voice their opinions? _____
_____

Which students do you think the teacher pays most attention to in this lesson? _____
_____
_____

Why do you think this is? _____
_____
_____

Which students do you consider work hard in, and outside, lessons?
_____

How well do you think you are doing in this lesson compared to other students _____
_____

Which students, in this class, would you compare yourself to in terms of academic achievement? ____
_____

Once you have left college are you planning to go to university, get a job or something else? (If something else please specify).
_____

What kind of degree or job are you planning to do? _____
_____

What do you see yourself doing in the future? _____

Figure 8

The questions themselves were carefully constructed so as to avoid influencing respondent's opinions. As little indication is given as possible as to the purpose of this research, knowledge of that purpose might bias the replies. This is the reason for the request on the teachers' questionnaire to use Christian names in answers, so that gender can be established but without calling gender to the respondent's attention. Only in the final question to teachers does a clue emerge to the issue under scrutiny, at a point when previous replies cannot be invalidated. The student questionnaire shows equal attention to avoiding leading or judgmental questions that reveal the researcher's intention.

The student's Results presentation is more patchy. Figure 9 shows an example of the presentational technique used for the non-participant observation of the four lessons. This is an overcrowded and generally unhelpful presentation. The categories the student used to log pupil behaviour (the left hand column) are important, but should be presented alongside the Methodological justification as a blank form. Here the task is to provide the reader with readily understandable data. The only section that achieves this in Figure 9 are the very bottom two figures of overall interaction by the teacher with male and female pupils. It is this brief but accurate and informative style that is needed. The student did achieve this as shown in Figure 10 of the overall results from the four observed classes. Here the reader can quickly see that in the secondary school the female teacher was nearer to equal with her time between the genders. However, importantly for this student's hypothesis, the male teacher's bias is actually in the female pupils' favour. Further, the Sixth Form College results show much greater bias towards the male students, particularly from the female teacher.

Figure 10 is an example of clear and penetrating presentation, although the student should briefly comment on what the data reveals in the manner done immediately above. This eliminates the problem of the reader looking through 20 or 30 diagrams or graphs before finding any explanation. Subsequently, in a final Evaluation, the student can comment across the research process. This summing up makes reference to the hypothesis/problematic, the methodology and the findings.

Results from the observation of a female teacher's class of 11/12 year olds in a secondary school

6 Boys / 6 Girls	No. of interactions		% of interactions	
	Male	Female	Male	Female
Told to get on with work	ЖЖ	||||	3.18	2.55
Told to sit down	||	|	1.27	0.64
Told to move	|||		1.91	–
Told to stop talking	||		1.27	–
Says "good", "well done"	|	|	0.64	0.64
Ask how getting on	ЖЖ	ЖЖ ЖЖ	3.18	6.37
Pick them when hands up	||	|||	1.27	1.91
Look at work	|	|||	0.64	1.91
Talk to unrelated to work	ЖЖ ЖЖ ЖЖ |	ЖЖ ЖЖ ЖЖ |	10.19	10.19
Pupil talks out	||||		2.55	–
Pupil asks for help	ЖЖ ЖЖ	ЖЖ ЖЖ |||	6.37	8.28
Pupil asks questions	ЖЖ ЖЖ ЖЖ ||	ЖЖ ЖЖ |||	10.83	8.28
Teacher helps pupil	ЖЖ ЖЖ ||	ЖЖ ЖЖ |||	7.64	8.28

6 Boys / 6 Girls	No. of times the teacher interacted as a %
Males	50.94
Females	49.05

Bearing in mind there were an equal amount of boys and girls there should have been a 50% interaction with both male and female pupils

Figure 9

Overall results from the four classes observed

	Overall interaction with a male as a %	Overall interaction with a female as a %
Secondary School with male teacher	40.18	59.18
Secondary School with female teacher	50.94	49.05
Sixth-Form College with male teacher	60.18	39.81
Sixth-Form College with female teacher	90.53	9.47

Figure 10

Results : Example 2

Student B produced a methodological justification and presentation of findings that were very qualitative. This was appropriate to her hypothesis which explored the experiences of the married woman compared with the expectations of the as yet unmarried woman. The extracts below illustrate how such qualitative findings can be accurately and understandably presented.

Extract from methodology section of Student B's project:

As I wished my results to be qualitative I used the in-depth interview method for the married women, and structured interviews for the unmarried women. I chose two different methods for the two groups as the married women would be relating experiences which had happened to them, whilst the unmarried women would have to imagine certain situations, which they would not previously have experienced.

The method

Agenda for married women – unstructured interviews
Listed below are some of the areas that were covered in the interviews:

- *who does what around the house*
- *general attitudes towards the mother role*
- *general attitude towards being called a housewife*
- *childcare*
- *housework*

Agenda for unmarried women – structured interviews

1 *Do you expect, hope or wish to marry? Why?*
2 *Do you expect, hope or wish to have children? Why?*
3 *Are you expected to help out at home with childcare or housework?*
4 *Will you and your partner intend to distribute household chores between you?*
5 *Who do you imagine will do the cooking: you or your partner?*
6 *Who will do the washing/laundry and ironing?*
7 *Who will stay at home to look after the children?*
8 *Who will go shopping?*
9 *Who will take responsibility for the garden?*
10 *Who will be most responsible for the hoovering, dusting and polishing?*
11 *Who will be most responsible for maintenance of the car?*
12 *Who will clean the toilet?*

The findings: extracts from the married sample

Mrs King*(aged 24).

Mrs King met her husband at 19, lived with him for two and a half years and then married after their first child was born.

Mrs King never worked after her first child was born, but did work prior to the birth. Mr King does not help out much at home, although Mrs King has hoped for some help, as she has two children and one on the way. Yet Mr King does perform the 'heavy duty work' such as car maintenance, whilst Mrs King 'does the lawn, but he does the garden'. Mrs King asks her eldest daughter to help her as Mrs King was expected to help when she was a child.

*Mrs Shaw *(aged 20).*

Mrs Shaw met her husband at 15, became pregnant at 16 and then married when she turned 18. They have a two year old daughter. Mrs Shaw has never worked full-time but takes seasonal work near Christmas. Mr Shaw works long hours during the week. However, he cooks dinner on Saturdays. During the week Mr Shaw goes out with friends a lot in the evening 'to help him relax'. Mrs Shaw does not expect her husband to help her in any other way as he works, nor does she ask. 'He wins the bread and I keep house.' Mrs Shaw would like to work in the future but thinks she will find it difficult to find any occupation that would fit in with her lifestyle as it is.

* note: as in all ethically aware studies, names have been changed by the student.

Unmarried women: extracted results

Below are the answers of the unmarried sample to the questions I asked about:

1 *All of the sample expected to get married, yet none of them could explain why. Most stated that they 'just wanted to'.*

2 *All of the sample, except one, hoped to have children. The person who 'didn't know' whether she would have children said she would try to have a career first. The remaining nine claimed that children would be 'fulfilling' or that childbirth was 'natural'. The sample looked on marriage and children as positive aspects of being female.*

3 *Eight out of the ten said that they were expected to help out at home. This involved 'vacuuming, dusting and washing up' through to making the beds. Even those two who said 'no', they were not expected to help, did help.*

Comments on Student B's presentation

This is an appropriate and accessible form of qualitative data presentation. Student B avoids becoming laboriously sidetracked in detailed answers of individual respondents. Without the need for any diagrams, she communicates the main feelings and views of her sample. This is where the skill of selecting the recurrent themes and concerns of a sample researched qualitatively can be successfully applied.

Results : Example 3

Another type of project approach produces more quantitative data, requiring different presentation. The following example is extracted from the project of

Student D exploring the relationship between educational attainment and social class. As the student explained in her Rationale:

My study aims to discover to what extent a person's social class can alter and influence their education, and whether their attitudes towards the education system and their future are a reflection of their class background. In order to do this the following hypothesis is going to be tested: 'A person's social class background is the main factor affecting educational attainment'.

The student goes on in her Methodology section to justify and explain her selection of a questionnaire methodology. The questionnaire is shown in Figure 11.

As the student explains:

A questionnaire is appropriate when testing the hypothesis 'A person's social class background is the main factor affecting educational attainment' because it allows results to be quantified and thus highlights any trends linking educational success with social class. It would not be possible to research this issue using methods such as participant observation because it is a quantitative type study.

Questionnaire

Name _____

Tutor Group _____

What is your father's occupation (or head of household)? _____

Which of the following best describes your housing? (Tick one from a and b.)

a Detached _____		**b** 5 or more bedrooms _____	
Semi-detached _____		3-4 bedrooms _____	
Terraced _____		2 bedrooms _____	
Flat _____		1 bedroom _____	

Do you have a bedroom of your own?_____

Which social class do you think you are?

Upper class _____	Lower middle/upper working class _____
Upper middle class _____	Working class _____
Middle class _____	Under class _____

In your GCSE Examinations which grades did you obtain in which subjects? _____

_____

Which of the following statements best fits your parents attitude towards your education?

Did not take any interest at all _____	Occasionally took an interest _____
Often encouraged me in my education _____	Pressurised me _____

Did your parents attend parents' evenings at your school?

Always _____	Never _____	Sometimes _____

What are your aspirations for the future? _____

_____

Figure 11

John Goldthorpe's social class scheme		
Classes	No	Description
Service class	1	Higher professionals, higher grade administrators, managers in large industrial concerns and large proprietors.
	2	Lower professionals, higher grade technicians, lower grade administrators, managers in small businesses and supervisors of non-manual employees.
Intermediate class	3	Routine non-manual – mainly clerical and sales personnel.
	4	Small proprietors and self-employed artisans.
	5	Lower grade technicians and supervisors of manual work.
Working class	6	Skilled manual workers.
	7	Semi-skilled and unskilled manual workers.

Table 8

A questionnaire was composed to suit the needs of the study. The respondent was asked to disclose information about their identity for purposes of further reference (especially on gender) if necessary; however, this was optional. Next people were questioned as to their father's occupation (or the head of household). This was necessary due to a person's social class being determined by their father's occupation and thus revealing their class position. This also ensures an even spread of respondents from each social class background, thus fairly representing each social class.

The classification of social class used to allocate people to a class category, by their father's occupation, is that of Goldthorpe's social class scheme (see table 8).

Three questions concerning housing were posed: these were aimed at gaining a basic representativeness of people's material background as this can greatly influence educational attainment and provides information on which assumptions can be made. For example, material assistance like books. Whether or not a person has a bedroom of their own is important, because it advantages or disadvantages them respectively by providing some pupils with somewhere to study privately.

The object of asking what social class a person believes themself to be in is that it reflects a person's lifestyle to a certain degree. If a person has a middle class lifestyle when they are in fact by definition really working class by their father's occupation, it may be that they believe they are middle class. This would thus result, in theory, in higher educational attainment as pupils are not oppressed by class inferiority (but not if they are materially working class).

GCSE examination results give definite levels of educational achievement which can be easily quantified and compared. Graded results represent a person's 'intelligence' level and are therefore both an efficient way of collecting data on attainment and are also representative of a person's ability.

The aim of enquiring whether or not parents encouraged pupils in their education is to find out whether or not many sociologists are justified in saying that parents' attitudes to their offspring affect educational success. It is said that middle class children are encouraged by their parents more than their working *class colleagues. This question reveals to what extent this is true.*

By asking the respondent to offer information about their aspirations for the future I hoped to establish whether or not there is a qualitative link between a person's achievements and aspirations. It also shows whether future aspirations are within the individual's present social class or are not limited by class boundaries.

The student has carefully explained here the reasons for using a questionnaire and also the thinking behind the individual questions asked. This justification enables the reader to understand the purpose behind the chosen method and how it relates to the type of research question being examined. The student's presentation of results is also commendable, as the two extracts in Figures 12 and 13 illustrate.

A table of comparison between social factors and educational achievement

GCSE Results	Class	Average house size	Parental encouragement Attitude	Parent evenings
56+	2 Service	3	2.5	2.5
51–55	3 Service 2 Intermediate 5 Working	2.9	3	2.7
46–50	5 Service 1 Intermediate 2 Working	3.25	3.125	2.875
40–45	1 Working	3	1	2
30–39	1 Working	3	3	3
20–29	N/A			

Figure 12

The student explains the rubric (how the table works) for Figure 12 underneath it.

It displays the number of people from each social class background within each of the achievement categories and averages for each bracket of housing size and parental encouragement, with higher averages being better. Thus, highlighting any direct links between social background (class, material background and parental attitudes) and educational attainment.

The student has clearly explained a concisely presented format to the reader. However, what is recommended is that the *interpretation* of the findings is presented alongside the data rather than in a summary at the end of ten or more diagrams, however helpfully they are explained. This student does evaluate the data in a high quality fashion in her final *evaluation* to the project, which is extracted below and should be read in conjunction with Figure 12. The learning point here is that this interpretation should be balanced between the Results and Evaluation sections, with the more evaluative conclusions which relate to the hypothesis explored in the Evaluation section.

Extract from evaluation on figure 12

The results of the questionnaire provide neither conclusive evidence that the hypothesis is correct or incorrect. Figure 12 suggests that initially social class background has caused differential attainment, with the achievers with over 56 points both within the service class [note: the student explains that grades A to G at GCSE were each given a point value so as to obtain one number to represent an individual's achievement level. Grade A = 7 points, grade B = 6 points and so on]. Further, the two lowest achievers have working class backgrounds. However, this pattern is not consistent with 50 % of people within the 51–55 bracket, who are in fact defined as working class. Perhaps, then, at the polarities of the class scale, achievement is affected by class but in the middle more flux takes place. Figure 12 also shows that average house size is not strongly connected to class and educational achievement, with people in the 46–50 grouping living in, as an average, larger houses than their higher achieving colleagues.

In the category of parental encouragement it appears that as far as parents' attitude towards their offspring goes, people within the 46–50 bracket were encouraged the most. One-third of these are from working class backgrounds and the remaining two-thirds are representing the intermediate and service classes. The 40–45 attainment level was represented solely by the working class who were not at all encouraged by parents, yet this is not so for the working class in the 30–39 category, being highly encouraged by parents but not achieving. For attendance at parents evening the pattern is very much the same. This supports the hypothesis because the level of parental encouragement does appear to be directly related to educational success. The most encouraged pupils were from middle class backgrounds, a majority of 66% in the 46–50 bracket. This agrees with Douglas [note: this sociologist's work on home – school social class influences was discussed in the student's Context] in that he believed social class background determines the degree of encouragement a person receives from their parents thus later affecting educational achievement.

The data in figure 12 is thus comprehensively and accurately analysed, then related explicitly to the student's initial hypothesis on the relationship between social class and educational attainment. This is partly the case in the following comments from this student's Evaluation which discusses figure 13. However, the student has neglected to explain all the findings presented in figure 13 – what has been overlooked? (Comments can be found in Chapter 6, p. 122.)

Figure 13 displays aspirations for the future and class mobility, showing that people are not limited by their social class in their ambitions. The proportion of the sample which are working class, generally wish to aspire upwards in the social system: they are not restricted by class boundaries.

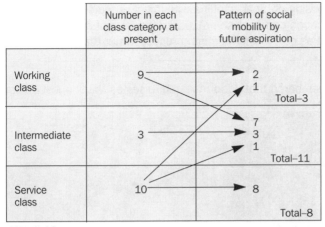

A table showing social mobility by future aspiration

Figure 13

Results and Evaluation Checklist

To conclude this section on the more practical aspects of final report presentation, the student should ensure the following:

- That the Results are presented in a separate section from the Methodological justification and the final Evaluation.

- That the format is appropriate to the data and to individually varying questions within the method. Some data may be presented graphically while another question's answers may require a prose summary such as the first example in this section on domestic labour.

- The data must be briefly explained as it is presented, rather than seeing the final Evaluation as the only place to comment on the findings.

- Seek clarity and user-friendliness, rather than a design award.

- Experiment with and test varying forms of data presentation. Show people the graph, figure or table, and see if they quickly understand it.

- Be intellectually honest. Always include aberrant or inconvenient data, commenting on how or why it may be so instead of trying to camouflage it.

- In evaluating at the close of the project, draw together problem–method conclusion(s) explicitly and with reference to:
  - the data found in the research
  - other existing sociological knowledge, aspects of which will have been explored in the Context earlier.

This is a difficult task but repays thoughtful attention. What has been learnt? Are the findings surprising or broadly in line with initial expectations? A considered and self-critical Evaluation can analyse practical difficulties of data collection and sample structure as part of the research process rather than lamented flaws.

It should be remembered that good research raises as many questions as it supplies answers.

ANSWERS AND COMMENTS ON EXERCISES

Participant Observation: Thompson and Williams: Comments (p. 21)

(i) Thompson chose participant observation because no other research method would have enabled unaltered observation of Hell's Angels behaviour. In the quite hostile police and public opinion atmosphere of 1965/66 (when Thompson was engaged in this study), the Hell's Angels were even more suspicious than at earlier times to 'outsiders', whether they be members of the public, journalists or even sociologists. Thompson had to, as he describes in the extract printed here from his book, become accepted by the Angels by hanging out with them and going through the process of joining. It is difficult to see how other methods, such as interviews or questionnaires could have worked given the hostile and deviant lifestyle of the group under study. Even overt participant observation would have been hazardous and probably have meant Thompson was excluded from much of the important interaction as he would have remained outside the group far more. Williams was similarly keen to explore the illegal world of drug-selling, and would not have progressed very far in his research by methods other than participant observation. However, in contrast to Thompson he took on an overt role, partly because of his age (Williams is a University Lecturer in New York City and the crack-cocaine sellers he studied were 'old' in the trade at 19 or 20) but also because he studied the sellers part-time, for two or three evenings a week over a three year period. Any covert role would therefore have been difficult.

(ii) Thompson describes in the extract some of the tensions that the Hell's Angels caused at his apartment, ultimately leading to his eviction. Elsewhere in the study he describes 'going over the high which, although not essential for joining the gang, certainly increased his credibility within it. Thompson also attended many Angels 'runs'; weekend trips away on bikes which frequently involved violence and drug and alcohol abuse. Williams describes in the extract some of the complications and restrictions of using PO in his study, pointing to the need to rmember events with the intention of recording them as fully and accurately as possible later. He also comments on the dangers involved.

In another sense, both researchers suffered from a more abstract drawback of PO, which is that they can only comment on what they observed – whilst only in one place or one group at a time, the results are necessarily small-scale and difficult to generalise from. However, both researchers (along with other sociologists who have used this method) argue this is more than compensated for by the high validity and immediacy of the data obtained.

(iii) Thompson worked with the general idea, already mentioned, that the media coverage of Hell's Angel behaviour was sensationalised and exaggerated. He made no specific predictions about this, however, and sought to infiltrate the groups involved in order to view events from their point of view. This has the distinct advantage that, without preconceptions as to Angel behaviour, he could watch it unfold and record it relatively dispassionately. Some of the most fascinating sections of an excellent book are Thompson's descriptions of Angel parties on 'runs', descending over several days into lawlessness and often, this behaviour involves willing participants rather than innocent members of the public. Equally, there are illegal acts perpetrated on non-Angel people, such as fights and rapes. This sort of discovery emerges from long days and nights of covert participation which do not really require, and are not especially methodologically helped by, having a specific hypothesis for the research.

Williams could equally only hazard the vaguest of descriptions of crack-cocaine selling before his study of it, and so would have arguably formed a hypothesis from media judgements and police reports, which may have been partial for many reasons. Until he had spent some months (part-time) observing the dealings he would not have been able to begin commenting objectively on the real world behind second hand accounts of drug-dealing, such as those in the media. Williams' book is actually a fine example of a piece of sociology that is fully ethnographic (as he explains in the extract), in that it is a full and detailed description of this underworld, made without judgements or abstract sociological heorising about its meanings or causes. He entered the underworld and conveyed a real feel for it to others. This is an advantage of both the ethnographic / observational method and its tendency to work from a broad framework of enquiry rather than the hypothetico-deductive statement and process.

Answers to Hypothesis Questionnaire Exercise (p. 26)

(i) The point here is that the student has used the terms 'television' and 'media' interchangeably. The media is the broader term that describes all forms of mass communication, and hence it covers the older forms of print such as books and newspapers (historically the earliest mass media, enabling one author to communicate with many readers) to the modern electronic means of mass communication this century: radio, film and television.

So as the mass media is, as Giddens has defined it, the 'Forms of communication, such as newspapers, magazines, radio or television designed to reach mass audiences' (Giddens, 1990) the student will have to distinguish television from this broader term. Television has become the dominant medium of this century but cannot be assumed to be the medium alone. Giddens also writes that: 'The influence of television...upon our lives is profound' as it does 'provide and shape much of the information which we utilise in our daily lives' (Giddens, 1990). Television still takes its place, and possibly has its influence alongside the other existing forms of mass media which people also use in their lives. As such, the student must distinguish this dominant medium (TV) from the mass media.

The impact this distinction has on the project could be considerable. In a negative sense, the student might continue to confuse the two terms and study a collection of media, mostly focused on television but variously bringing in film and so on. This would be acceptable if intended, but poor research if the consequence of loose definitions at the hypothesis stage. In a positive sense, the student might specify television as the main object of study from within the mass media, and justify such a decision in the context and methodology sections of the project, because previous sociological work has indicated television has the primary influence in its sexual and violent content. This illustrates the high importance of accurate sociological terminology in the hypothesis statement.

(ii) This tentative hypothesis statement could be more accurately re-phrased as something like the following:

Aspects of television content can make viewers sad or frightened, showing the direct effect this medium has on its audience.

With this phrasing of the hypothesis, the particular form of the media chosen for study (television) is pinpointed and stays consistent throughout the proposition statement. Further, words such as 'aspects' and 'viewers' are more descriptive uses of language for a statement which should be setting the parameters for the research concisely. It may often prove necessary to re-phrase a hypothesis several times before a satisfactory working version is arrived at.

(iii) The sociologically and/or methodologically problematic words here are:

- sad   - aroused
- frightened   - making
- violent

The first four of these are highly problematical as they are open to misinterpretation or subjectivity. For example, in Taylor and Mullen's *Uninvited Guests* study (1986), in which a sample of 3000 viewers were asked their responses to a wide range of television content from news to drama and film, many viewers claimed to have become 'sad' or 'frightened' at certain times when watching television. The problem with such data is that individual meanings are attached to the response: what one person means by 'frightened' could vary considerably from another's. Does it mean to have had a disturbed night of sleep following the programme? Does it mean to have temporarily looked away from the screen at a tense or physically aggressive moment?

The complications of these definitions can be further illustrated by considering the terms 'violent' and 'aroused'.

Researchers into the possible effects of television violence have encountered methodological difficulties in this area of definition, sometimes with quite serious consequences for the validity of the data gathered. One of the more famous studies that purports to have empirically proved a correlation between violent portrayals on television and increases in actual viewer involvement in violent acts is William Belson's *Television Violence and the Adolescent Boy* (1978). Although Belson collected data from 1565 boys in in-depth interviews, his finding that viewing increases participation in violence is strongly contested on the grounds that suspect definitions of violence were employed in the research process. As just one example to measure how violent the boys' actual behaviour was, Belson asked them to state what acts they had committed: this clearly leaves the possibility of not confessing to some acts or to inventing others for the sake of 'image'. In addition, Belson categorised acts on a scale of seriousness, the most serious including diverse forms of offence from vandalising telephone boxes to intentionally hitting someone else in the face with a bottle. As Murdock and McCron subsequently argued (1979), this approach groups together acts of violence of different moral order, so making their comparison and link to television viewing tentative.

Similarly, the notion of a viewer becoming 'aroused' through television content of a sexual nature is controversial to research. While some feminist writers such as Cockburn and Loach have stated that images of women that present them as available or as sexual objects do have a correlation with sexual crimes against women, other writers from the same theoretical standpoint have stressed the media's tendency to present narrow roles for women (housewife; mother; unfaithful woman) and to reinforce the feminine role (Ferguson, 1983: McRobbie, 1985). There is hence no one agreement on the effects of such content, nor on operational definitions of concepts such as 'arousal'.

None of these are impenetrable methodological barriers. What such existing work illustrates is the crucial role term and concept definition plays in the research process. Lastly here is the word 'making', which asserts that a correlation (or causal relationship) exists between the two variables of viewing and then committing, for example, violent acts. Would a researcher have to assume, for instance, that the causing of a response in the viewer necessitates a short time-lag? Is someone only likely to be violent shortly after watching content that may incite them to such acts, or could a more cumulative effect be operating? This has been referred to as the 'brutalisation' of our cultural life through having each evening's viewing content contain at least some violence? The use of the word 'making' here assumes correlations of one of these kinds.

(iv) The suggested possible methods on this student's hypothesis questionnaire are:

- interview
- questionnaire
- diaries

In addition to this, the student has correctly noted that participant observation and case studies would be complicated in this chosen research area, as small samples and intrusion difficulties arise. However, other possibilities may be:

- Group discussion with a sample of viewers, perhaps before and after watching brief videos of examples of arguably violent or sexual television content.
- Content analysis could be employed. This is a technique whereby the researcher analyses the images and messages of a media treatment for its meaning and potential impact – very interesting work has been done in this way by several researchers; the Glasgow University Media Group (GUMG) on news bias (1976, 1980 and 1982), Ros Gill on images of

women (1988) and so on. The basic methodological weakness of content analysis is the possibility of subjectivity, as the researcher is deciding on meaning and probable message.

- There is the option of conducting the research in a longitudinal fashion, following the viewing experiences of a sample over three or four months (any longer would impose time difficulties on an A level project) to investigate any cumulative effect such as that referred to at the end of point 3.

It is instructive, then, to attempt to consider as full a range of methodologies as possible and subsequently select from them.

Summary of exercise

This exercise has been to demonstrate the importance of constructing a hypothesis and initial ideas on methodology with attention to accuracy that will prevent problems occurring later in the project. Close consultation with the course tutor is strongly advised to check points such as those raised in the example used above.

Answers to Student A B C Hypotheses Exercise (p. 34)

(i) As is observed in the comments immediately following Student A's hypothesis, the proposition is stated quite categorically as seeking a causative link between types of gender-biased interaction in the classroom and lower female attainment in schooling. There is the need, then, to prove three related sociological points within this project:

- that males receive more interaction with teachers than females
- that females underattain relative to their male peers
- that the former is the cause of the latter.

This search for causation is both a strength and a possible source of complication for this hypothesis. There is, to raise only one example, a well-documented tendency for the socialization of boys and girls to be markedly different in western cultures within the family – this may exert a lasting influence on gender behaviour even prior to schooling, which then makes it complicated to separate the precise cause of differential gender attainment. It would be equally reasonable to suggest the cause lay within family structures and parental role models, as within only the education system. However, Student A received considerable credit from the marking scheme for proposing quite a sophisticated relationship between the three factors outlined above, and enquiring into their interrelationship in a sensitive manner.

Student B's hypothesis seeks to establish the feelings of women on conjugal roles.

This does contain the intrinsic difficulty of asking people to imagine future arrangements – people are often inaccurate in responding to sociologists questions about what they are currently doing or have done in the past, so any research involving asking people for possible projected arrangements might be compounding these reporting difficulties. Nevertheless, correctly acknowledged and allowed for sympathetically at the interview stage, Student B was able to justify this chosen approach in her methodology section.

(ii) Student A – choosing the method

Student A's choice of method is appropriately fashioned to the chosen hypothesis. A blend of primary and secondary data is required, as is a mixture of observational (for the classroom interaction aspect of the hypothesis) techniques and quantitative data for the comparison of levels of attainment for boys and girls. This is an example of how methodologies that, strictly delineated, originate in differing sociological traditions can be effectively combined.

Student A – gathering the data

The key with this project at the data-gathering stage was the time and care that was invested, spending several weeks gaining the observational data alone (although the student was obviously not in classrooms for all this time, what it indicates is many visits to the observed institutions rather than just one, which is a problem with Student C's data-gathering).

Student B – choosing the method

Student B correctly employs a highly qualitative research tool (interviews) and pays particularly commendable attention to the sampling procedure used to obtain a desirable sample for interview. This reinforces the point made on page 26 that integration of the hypothesis with appropriate methods is essential to a well-balanced and coherent project, and that the sampling procedure within the method selection is also important.

Student B has specified certain characteristics she needs to have in her sample (women aged between 16 and 26, the married ones of whom should have experience of a child) so that she is asking questions of a group of women with experiences relevant to the hypothesis on changing conjugal roles.

Student B – gathering the data

This is extremely comprehensive, making Student B's analysis of data subsequently quite exhaustive. A mass of information was accumulated from some 30 hours or so of total interviewing time, which is certainly an impressive time investment for the A level project. It also means the data can be generalised from with some confidence, as this sample size and interview length replicates that of full and quite renowned sociological studies. For example, Elizabeth Bott's study of conjugal role arrangements involved interviewing twenty couples (Bott, 1971).

Good practice of this kind will gain high reward from the mark scheme.

Student C – choosing the method

Student C has chosen appropriate methods (non-participant observation and questionnaire) but has made the mistake of having a tiny sample base: one class, one teacher, observed once. Hence the results are not likely to give much confidence that anything other than very particular conclusions can be drawn from such a limited study.

The case of Student C here does illustrate the following:

a The hypothesis must be a statement not a question.
b The chosen methodology cannot be assumed to integrate with the topic area and hypothesis – these connections must be made explicitly by the candidate in the Methodology section of the project.
c The recommended word lengths for each section of the final submitted project must be very close to those suggested in Chapter 1.

Student C – gathering the data

Student C's approach will not yield sufficiently detailed or high quality data for A level work. One visit to the school by Student C was methodologically unsound as it could have been an untypical day in all sorts of ways (different lessons on different days is quite a common primary school pattern, for instance).

It also compounded the fact that the chosen methodology could only deal with relatively small total samples anyway. This arguably makes it even more important for data validity for the student to observe either the same class several times, or to observe several different classes and hence be addressing an inherent weakness of qualitative research of this kind.

Summary of exercise

Students A and B have quite sophisticated hypotheses and have sensitively applied appropriate research techniques in the data-gathering phase. Importantly, in addition to this they have noted why they chose their respective methodologies in a clear effort to justify their applicability to their study.

Student C has either run into time difficulties and rushed the data-gathering, has not understood the Exam Board's requirements or is guilty of insufficient motivation to produce rigorous research. All these are and should be avoidable.

Marks and Comments on the Rationale Exercise (pp. 36–7)

Student B's Rationale

This Rationale falls into mark range 13–17, with a mark of 14 awarded. Below are indicated the good elements of this Rationale and the areas where there could be improvement:

Positive elements

- At approximately 450 words this is much closer to a full Rationale.
- It sets a much more comprehensive and detailed framework for the hypothesis than the Rationale by Student B. There is good detail on Tiger and Fox, Hartman and Willmott and Young.
- There is a clear and accurate explanation of the chosen methodology.

Student B gained 70% for her project overall, and a B grade in the final A level results.

Areas for improvement

- The student could be more explicit on the aims of the enquiry and predicting what will be found
- There could be a little more explanation immediately above and below the actual hypothesis statement about the hypothesis. The statement is placed between a body of sociological work and the methods description, and although it is not 'free-floating' it could be 'located' in the progression of the text a bit more.

These comments indicate that Student B has produced a very comprehensive and impressive Rationale, omitting only a couple of possible aspects that could be further developed. It is hopefully apparent from the above exercise that the elements in a full and comprehensive Rationale are:

- Mention of preliminary observations and why the area of study is chosen.
- A fairly brief outline of the theoretical Context the area of study falls within.
- The hypothesis statement.
- Explanation of the hypothesis statement.
- Predictions on the expected outcome of the research.
- An overall word length of around 600.

Student C's Rationale

This Rationale falls into mark range 9–12, with a mark of 9 awarded. Below are indicated the good aspects of this Rationale and the areas where improvement could occur:

Positive elements

- Good reference to Spender and Clarricoates, although this could be done in greater detail.
- It is clear on the preliminary observation and the aims of the enquiry (to uncover gender bias).

Areas for improvement

- The occasional odd phrasing needs attention; for example, the hypothesis statement itself or such sentences as '...to see if the teacher was making any stereotypings amongst the children'. It is possible to see Student C's meaning here, but a clearer phrasing might be: '...to see if the teacher formed any stereotypes of the children which then affected them'. This point is more significant in the overall Context of Student C's project, as this kind of slightly unhelpful phrasing occurred frequently enough to hinder the reader.
- The brief mention of the methods is too vague. The student intends to ask the children 'a few questions', and to have 'an interview or questionnaire for the teacher'. This is insufficiently defined for an opening statement of aims and intention.
- The overall Rationale length is approximately 260 words, and it should really be nearer to 600. The extra words could have usefully been applied to:

  - detail more the sociological context of the study (other sociologists than just Spender and Clarricoates, important although their work is, have studied interaction in the classroom
  - explain the methodology more clearly
  - provide more detail to the actual hypothesis statement: why does this require classroom observation? What will be discovered?

These comments indicate that a relatively sound Rationale could be significantly improved by attention to the above points.

   This student gained 40% overall for her project, but a grade N in the final A level results.

Comments on the Stanley Cohen Interview Schedule (pp. 59–60)

Cohen's interview schedule has the distinct strength of avoiding prejudicial or judgemental phrases. Notice how frequently he uses the phrase 'this sort of thing'. This is to avoid placing suggestions of disapproval before his interviewee, who will have been a local person coincidentally observing random violence nearby. Cohen also makes careful use of the word 'handle' ('handling' ; 'handled'), again to allow freedom of thought for the respondent to police reaction to the mod/rocker behaviour.

   On the negative side, this could appear vague to a questioned member of the public, and at least one question is difficult to understand accurately (question 6

– what is the difference between (a) and (b)?). It is also difficult to judge how much Cohen's preamble may have reassured his respondents, or how suggestive his probing was with the final question. This is why those advocating a more empirical / positivist methodology lean towards the greater rigidity of the focused or structured interview.

Answers from the Kinsey Institute Questionnaire (pp. 62–3)

1 f or g is correct
2 d or e is correct
3 True
4 False
5 True

Statistics Example (p. 81)

1 479

2 Essentially, the numbers of males dying each year has fallen from a high point of 40,224 at the turn of the century to around 30,000 in the last decade. This represents a substantial decline in the death rate, given the male population in total in Scotland will have risen considerably 1900 to 1990. The figures thus reflect the increased average longevity achieved this century – more males are living longer.

3 **a** A dramatic decline in infant mortality is indicated by these statistics. The numbers dying in infancy between 1900 and 1922 are really quite high, measured in the several thousand. The situation improves rapidly post-war (after 1945), such that today only a few hundred babies are lost each year.

    b In reverse to the patterns analysed thus far, the figures for the very elderly (85 +) show an improving longevity in the population if the total deaths themselves increase. This indicates that more people are living long enough to die in their late eighties. A figure of under 1000 deaths per annum in this age category at the turn of the century becomes over 3000 per year since 1988, having risen steadily through the century.

4 Many environmental and medical improvements this century would account for these changing death rate figures.

    For instance, from 1899 Rowntree's poverty surveys in York, pioneering social analysis of their time, showed the link between poverty, poor diet and ill health/early mortality. The nutritional needs of the general population, particularly important to the very young and the elderly, have improved dramatically since 1900. Around 40% of the 40,224 people who died in 1900–02 were over 45 years of age, meaning their nutritional and health habits would date back to the 1850s at least. Hence, the gains made on diet and basic healthcare early this century show through from the 1930s onwards.

The current health and welfare apparatus in the United Kingdom dates from 1945, when the Beveredge Report set up the modern welfare state. The long held ideal (and actuality) of free at point-of-use health care, free school meals for the poor and so on have obviously contributed enormously to the death rate decline and increased longevity after the 1940s. These figures, then, reflect and indicate social policies from another era.

5   Females live longer. Since the 1930s, the number of females dying aged 85 + has been approximately twice that of males, suggesting there have been many more females in this age category to die. Female deaths in the 75–84 age range are also somewhat ahead of males.

Explanations for this vary. Women may be biologically stronger than males; certainly, women suffer far less from heart disease and heart attacks, which remain the single largest cause of male death.

6   Yes, it is generally reliable. The source, denoted at the bottom right of the table, is the Scottish General Register Office which records deaths. Very few deaths will remain undetected or go unnoticed in any one year, so we can assume the actual numbers are really quite accurate.

The compilers themselves hint at one small methodological issue in the bottom left hand side of the table. Some individuals where the date of birth is unsure (probably more common earlier on this century before accurate record keeping) are included in the total column. This means the total column should contain slightly more deaths than the breakdown of individual age categories. The inaccuracy to the general picture of each age category would be extremely small.

Comments on Historical Documents Exercise (pp. 84–5)

a   This query lies at the heart of criticisms of the documentary research method. Did the people recording the data conceal anything unflattering? With war this is particularly problematic, as cowardice, desertion and failure are often disguised or covered up in wartime so as not to deflate morale. Women who objected to the American Civil War or who tried to keep their male loved ones from fighting may not appear in these histories of the female contribution. In this sense, women's appearance in war history may be as ideologically framed as that of men's.

Those recording events at a time in history often have their own particular motives. The American Civil War was the first war to be photographed. It is now known that some of the most famous and harrowing of these photographs were carefully composed after battles, the dead being moved into poignant positions to make a better battle photograph. If this was done with the visual record of the war, it is entirely possible that some of the written accounts suffer from selectivity or alteration to look better for that side in the conflict.

Caution must be applied, therefore, to interpretation from documentary sources.

b *A document of life* is a record of one person's life in considerable detail. Its purpose is to show how the social circumstances studied in sociology, such as class, gender or race, have an impact through a life.

The *historical document* is attempting something different. Its task is to convey events, usually of a group of people, from a particular time. From this record of events the contemporary sociologist tries to interpret the key social trends, norms and values of the time.

Both methods collect historical information, but documents of life do so with the distinctly micro-sociological intention of studying the life of an individual. Elshtain's war documents above contain some details of individual lives but the overall picture is of a revised version of women's role in wartime.

Student Data Presentation: Comments (p. 108)

Comments on figure 13

The student has not sufficiently analysed these findings, although the presentation in figure 13 is original and readily understandable.

Both Heath 1981 and Marshall 1988 have commented on the high levels of class self-recruitment revealed by their social mobility studies (Heath, *A. Social Mobility*, Fontana, Glasgow, 1981; Marshall, G., Newby, H., Rose, D. and Vogler, C. *Social Class in Modern Britain*, Hutchinson, London, 1988). This means there is a marked tendency for many members of a social class to be of that origin themselves at birth, indicating low levels of social mobility generally. In figure 13 it is seen that 100% of the intermediate sample and 80% of the service sample aspire to retain their class of origin.

The student has overlooked this. Also overlooked are the curiously muted ambitions of her (precariously small) intermediate sample, all of whom only wish to stay in their class of origin. Further, none of the upwardly aspirant working class sample (7 of the 9 individuals) wish for service sector jobs. This illustrates perhaps restricted ambition and the acknowledged problem from as long ago as Glass (1954) that long range upward social mobility is generally very limited (Glass, D.V. *Social Mobility in Britain*, RKP, London, 1954).

The point to note from this additional interpretation of Figure 13 data is two-fold:

1 The student overlooked points, probably through focusing narrowly on the educational angle rather than considering the findings of social mobility studies. She is, after all, exploring the link between the two in her project by way of the concept of class.
2 Clearly presented data is not, alone, sufficient. It must be fully analysed and discussed.

*B*IBLIOGRAPHY

Andrew, S. and Heaton, T. 'Coursework – The Students' Perspective', *Sociology Review* Vol 2, No 4, p. 26–8, Philip Allan Publishers Ltd, 1993.

Ball, S. *Beachside Comprehensive*, Cambridge University Press, 1981.
Barker, E. *The Professional Stranger*, Open University Press, 1981.
Becker, H. *Outsiders*, The Free Press, 1963.
Berger, P.L. Berger, B. and Kellner, H. *The Homeless Mind:Modernisation and Consciousness*, Penguin, 1974.
Bilton, A. et al (2nd Edition) *Introductory Sociology*, MacMillan, 1989.
Blumer, H. *In Critiques of Research in the Social Sciences*: An Appraisal of Thomas and Znaniecki's *The Polish Peasant in Europe and America*, Transaction Books, 1979).
Blumer, H. Frazier, E.F. (1967) *Negro Youth at the Crossways; their personality development in the Middle States*; 1979, Shocken Books, originally published in 1940.
Bott, E. *Family and Social Network*, Tavistock, 1971.
Brunt, R. *Good Morning Britain*, pp. 60–73 in Goodwin, G. and Whannel, G. (eds) *Understanding Television*, Routledge, 1992.

Chambliss, B. *Box Man*: *A Professional Thief's Journal* (by Harry King as told to Bill Chambliss), Harper and Row, 1972.
Cicourel, A.V. *The Social Organisation of Juvenile Justice*, Heinemann, 1976.
Cockburn, C. and Loach, L. *In Whose Image*, in Curran, J., Ecclestone, J., Oakley, G. and Richardson, A. (eds) *Bending Reality; The State of the Media*, Pluto Press, 1986.
Cohen, S. *Folk Devils and Moral Panics*, Paladin, 1973.

Delamont, S. and Stubbs, M. (eds). *Explorations in Classroom Behaviour*, Wiley, 1976.
Douglas, J. W. B. *The Home and The School*, MacGibbon and Kee, 1964.
Durkheim, E. *Suicide*; *A Study in Sociology*, RKP, 1970 (originally published in 1897).

Elshtain, J .B., *Women and War*, Brighton Harvester, 1987.
Eysenck, H.J. and Nias, D. Sex, *Violence and the Media*, Temple Smith, 1978.

Ferguson, *Forever Feminine*; *Women's Magazines and the Cult of Femininity*, Heinemann, 1983.

Garfinkel, H. *Studies in Ethnomethodology*, Prentice-Hall, 1967.
Gavron, H. *The Captive Wife: Conflicts of Housebound Mothers*, Routledge, 1966.
Giddens, A. *Sociology*, Polity Press. Gill, R. (Sept. 1988) 'Altered Images; Women in the Media', *Social Studies Review*, Philip Allan Publishers Ltd, 1989.
Glasgow University Media Group, *Bad News*, RKP, 1976.
Glass, D.V. *Social Mobility in Britain*, RKP, 1954.
Goffman, E. *Asylums*, Penguin, 1968.

Goldthorpe, J.H., Lockwood, D., Bechhofer, F. and Platt, J. *The Affluent Worker in the Class Structure*, Cambridge University Press, 1969.

Griffin, C. *Typical Girls?*, RKP, 1985.

Hakim, C. *Secondary Analysis in Social Research*, Allen and Unwin, 1982.

Haralambos, M. *Sociology; A New Approach*, Causeway Press, 1986.

Haralambos, M. *Sociology; Themes and Perspectives*, Unwin Hyman.

Hargreaves, D. (1967) *Social Relations in a Secondary School*, Routledge, 1990.

Hartman, H. 'Capitalism, Patriarchy and Job Segregation by Sex', in Blaxall, M and Reagan, B. (eds) *Women and the Workplace*, University of Chicago Press, 1976.

Heath, A. *Social Mobility*, Fontana, 1981.

Hite, S. *The Hite Report on Female Sexuality*, Macmillan, 1976.

Hite, S. *The Hite Report on Male Sexuality*, New York, Alfred A. Knopf, 1981.

Hite, S. *The Hite Report on Love, Passion and Emotional Violence*, Macdonald 1991.

Howe, N.F. 'Go Forth and Research', *Sociology Review*, Vol 2, No 1, Philip Allan Publishers Ltd, 1992.

Jennings, H. and Madge, C. (eds) *Mass Observation Day Survey May 12th 1937*, Faber and Faber, 1987.

Kinsey, A.C. *Sexual Behaviour in the Human Male*, W.B. Saunders, 1948.

Kinsey, A.C. *Sexual Behaviour in the Human Female*, W.B. Saunders, 1953.

La Piere, R.T. 'Attitudes versus actions', *Social Forces* Vol.13, 1934.

Lewis, O. *Five Families*, Basic Books, New York, 1959.

Lewis, O. (1970) *A Death in the Sanchez Family*, Secker and Warburg.

Liebow, E. *Tally's Corner*, Little Brown, 1967.

Malinowski, M. *Magic, Science and Religion and Other Essays*, Souvenir Press, 1982.

Marshall, G., Newby, H., Rose, D. and Vogler, C. *Social Class in Modern Britain*, Hutchinson, 1988.

Mass, S. and Kuypers, J.A. *From Thirty to Seventy: A 40 Year Long Study of Adult Lifestyles and Personality*, Jossey-Bass, 1974.

Matza, D. *Delinquency and Drift*, John Wiley and Sons, 1964.

Mayntz, R. *Introduction to Empirical Sociology*, Penguin, 1976.

Mead, M. *Coming of Age in Somoa; A Study of Adolescence and Sex in Primitive Societies*, Penguin, 1971.

Merton, R.K. *Social Theory and Social Structure*, The Free Press, 1968.

Midwinter, E. *British Gas Survey On Ageing*, British Gas plc, 1991.

Moore, F. *Women of the War; Their Heroism and Self-Sacrifice*, Scranton, 1867.

Morrison, M. *Methods in Sociology*, Longman Group Limited, 1986.

Oakley, A. *The Sociology of Housework*, Martin Robertson, 1974.

O'Donnell, M. (3rd Edition) *A New Introduction to Sociology*, Thomas Nelson and Sons, 1992.

O'Donnell, M. (3rd Edition) *A New Introductory Reader in Sociology*, Thomas Nelson and Sons, 1993.

Pahl, R. *Divisions of Labour*, Blackwell, 1984.

Patrick, J. *A Glasgow Gang Observed*, Eyre Methuen, 1973.

Pawson, R. *A Measure for Measures; A Manifesto for Empirical Sociology*, Routledge, 1989.

Phillips, D.L. *Knowledge From What?*, Rand McNally, 1971.

Platt, J. 'Case Studies; Their Uses and Limitations', *Sociology Review*, Vol 2, No 3, Philip Allan Publishers, 1993.

Plummer, K. *Documents of Life:An Introduction to the Problems and Literature of a Humanistic Method*, George Allen and Unwin Ltd, 1983.

Reinisch, J.M. and Beasley, R. *The Kinsey Institute New Report on Sex*, Penguin, 1990.

Samuel, R. *East End Underworld:Chapters in the Life of Arthur Harding*. Routledge and Kegan Paul, 1981.

Searle, C. *Your Daily Dose; Racism and The Sun,* Campaign for Press and Broadcasting Freedom, 1989.

'Social Trends', Government Statistical Service, quoted in Slattery, M. *Official Statistics*, Tavistock Publications, 1986.

Spender, D. *Invisible Women; Schooling Scandal*, Women's Press, 1983.

Stanworth, M. *Gender and Schooling*, Hutchinson, 1983.

Strauss, A. and Glasner, B. *Anguish: A Case History of a Dying Trajectory*, Martin Robertson, 1977.

Taylor, L. and Mullen, R. *Uninvited Guests*, Coronet Books.

Thomas, W.I. and Znaniecki, F. (1958) *The Polish Peasant in Europe and America,* 1987; Dover Publications (original editions published 1918-1920).

Thompson, H. *Hell's Angels*, Penguin, 1966.

Tiger, L. and Fox, R. *The Imperial Animal*, Secker and Warburg, 1972.

Warde, A. 'Domestic Divisions of Labour', *Social Studies Review*, Philip Allan Publishers Ltd, 1988.

Weber, M. *The Protestant Ethic and the Spirit of Capitalism*, George Allen and Unwin, 1930.

Whyte, W.F. (2nd Edition) *Street Corner Society*, University of Chicago Press, 1955.

Williams, T. *Cocaine Kids*, Bloomsbury Publishing Ltd, 1990.

Willmott, P. and Young, M. *Family and Kinship in East London*, Penguin, 1962.

INDEX